D0104763

Praise for

A FOREVER FAMILY

"Scheer's determination to 'be the father that I never had' while helping kids in the flawed foster care system will inspire, educate, and astound readers."

—*Publishers Weekly* (starred review)

"In an unsparingly honest and warmhearted book, the author moves the narrative along with vivid details that are alternately joyful and sorrowful to read . . . A heartwarming, hopeful memoir brimming with humanitarianism and compassion."

—*Kirkus Reviews*

"The personal journeys of Rob, Reece, and their four children are emotionally engaging, and their firsthand perspective on foster care and adoption, with the added dimension of them being a same-sex couple, may spark serious discussion of a complex, challenging topic."

—*Booklist*

A FOREVER FAMILY

Fostering Change
One Child at a Time

ROB SCHEER

with *Jon Sternfeld*

GALLERY BOOKS

JETER PUBLISHING

New York   London   Toronto   Sydney   New Delhi

Gallery Books / Jeter Publishing
An Imprint of Simon & Schuster, Inc.
1230 Avenue of the Americas
New York, NY 10020

Copyright © 2018 by Scheer Focus, LLC

Photograph on page 255 © Joyce Smith Photography.
Photograph on the left on page 277 courtesy of American Girl.
All other photographs courtesy of the author.

All the names in the book have been changed, except my own and those
of most of my immediate family and my friends Ricky and Rodger.
Dialogue is re-created from memory.

All rights reserved, including the right to reproduce this book or portions thereof in any
form whatsoever. For information, address Gallery Books Subsidiary Rights Department,
1230 Avenue of the Americas, New York, NY 10020.

First Gallery Books trade paperback edition May 2019

GALLERY BOOKS and colophon are registered trademarks of
Simon & Schuster, Inc.

For information about special discounts for bulk purchases, please contact Simon &
Schuster Special Sales at 1-866-506-1949 or business@simonandschuster.com.

The Simon & Schuster Speakers Bureau can bring authors to your live event.
For more information or to book an event, contact the Simon & Schuster Speakers
Bureau at 1-866-248-3049 or visit our website at www.simonspeakers.com.

Interior design by Bryden Spevak

Manufactured in the United States of America

10 9 8 7 6 5 4 3 2 1

The Library of Congress has cataloged the hardcover edition as follows:

Names: Scheer, Rob, author. | Sternfeld, Jon, author.
Title: A forever family : fostering change one child at a time / Rob Scheer with Jon
    Sternfeld.
Description: New York, NY : Gallery Books, [2018] | Includes bibliographical references.
Identifiers: LCCN 2018022910 | ISBN 9781501196638 (hardcover) | ISBN
    9781501196645 (trade paper) | ISBN 9781501196652 (ebook)
Subjects: LCSH: Scheer, Rob. | Foster parents—Biography. | Foster children—Biography.
    | Adoptees—Biography.
Classification: LCC HQ759.7 .S33 2018 | DDC 306.874—dc23
LC record available at https://lccn.loc.gov/2018022910

ISBN 978-1-5011-9663-8
ISBN 978-1-5011-9664-5 (pbk)
ISBN 978-1-5011-9665-2 (ebook)

For all the children in foster care,

those who are entering the system, and those who are aging out

CONTENTS

CONTENTS

A FOREVER FAMILY

INTRODUCTION

I always wanted a traditional family. This didn't necessarily mean we all looked alike, or had the same blood, or even the same name. Just that we were a family bonded through love. That vision I carried seemed like something that so many others had, through no doing of their own. But for me, a family remained out of reach for a long time. It took work. It took a choice.

I grew up never feeling safe, never thinking of a single place as home, carrying the few things I could call my own in a trash bag. I suffered abuse at the hands of my biological parents, my stepfather, my foster father, neighbors, cousins, boyfriends, and strangers. It all took a toll, making me feel worthless, like I deserved to be treated poorly. As I grew up and struggled through depression, homelessness, and battles with drug addiction, I never felt anything resembling love. I dated men who were abusive because I thought that's what love was. I hadn't learned any other way.

Despite my longing for a family, I was certain I'd never find love, positive I would never be married or be able to become a father. My path seemed clearly laid out for me: dropout, convict, addict, forgotten, homeless, and alone. A tragic story, a life ended too soon, not even worth covering in the newspaper.

I spent decades carrying demons, baggage from my past that weighed me down and never let me be free. I am fifty-one years old now, and I still feel them.

But something in my spirit refused to die, refused to give up hope. I had no evidence, but something more like faith that life had very different plans for me.

Though I was kicked out of my foster home soon after my eighteenth birthday, forced to sleep in my car and public bathrooms, I made it through high school. From there I went into the military and then into a series of office jobs. I diligently worked my way up and found a measure of stability, but I never shared what happened to me. I kept my story wrapped up tight and to myself. A feeling latched onto me that I couldn't shake, of fear, of shame, of low self-worth.

Then I met Reece. I fell in love with him, and we decided to start a family. We adopted our four children and made a home. I changed my story. I became something else: not a victim, not a statistic, not a cautionary tale, not a pity case. I became a loving husband and father and someone who was able to—and wanted to—give back.

Though I was the product of a broken family and a shattered system, love changed the course of my life. It is my hope that in telling my story I might be able to help others.

I had first been set on adopting overseas, not willing to again face the system that broke me, but Reece convinced me it was my duty to seek out those kids who were experiencing what I had. To change their story.

We took in four foster kids from the DC system—who all showed up with their minimal things in trash bags. The sight of those trash bags brought back all the pain of my childhood and my time in the system. I never wanted the children to go back in there, so we petitioned to adopt them. The system and courts felt that because Reece and I were white, we couldn't be suitable parents to African American children and because we were gay we shouldn't be allowed to be parents at all.

But our children just wanted love. I just wanted love. We needed each other.

●

All of us are constantly reinventing ourselves. We have that opportunity each and every day.

We are a combination of all our choices in life, and I made the choice to never let a horrific childhood become a tragic adulthood. I can do nothing about my past; but every day, I make a point of living as best as I can, as kindly as I can, and with as much grace as I can.

I can't teach anyone how to be gay, or how to be a white father to black children. We're all made of a different cloth; it is our love that binds us all together.

In 2013 I started Comfort Cases, an organization that makes sure that foster children never have to suffer the indignity and inhumanity of living out of trash bags. We pack backpacks for these children that let them know that we, as a community, love them and we want them. It's a message I would have given anything to hear during my difficult years growing up.

•

My hope is that *A Forever Family* will inspire all those out there who feel stuck or as though no one cares for them. If you are out there, I assure you that you are not alone. I am here. *We are here.* Maybe this book can also empower all the others who want to help but feel like they can't or don't know how. And of course, I would love to live in a world where our story—the story of my family and me—is no longer rare.

It is my mission to give hope and comfort to those currently struggling with many of the issues I dealt with: abuse, foster care, drugs, living in the closet, the pain before and the thrill after legalized gay marriage, and the trials of adoption. These are things that need to be part of a national conversation. Those who suffer should never feel alone or do so in silence.

1

WHAT WE DON'T TALK ABOUT

June 2008

One Saturday morning, Reece and I were sitting on the leather couch in our living room, drinking coffee and rubbing the sleep out of our eyes. Bailey, our liver-spotted Dalmatian, was next to us on the rug. We had been at a cocktail party the night before that had gone well past midnight. In those days, we were sociable creatures who went out quite a bit with our wonderful group of friends. We'd go out late, stay out late, and sleep in late.

Reece sat across from me, with a shiny bald head, piercing blue eyes, and silver hoops in his ears. Gentle and nurturing, fashionable and independent, he is the love of my life. We had been together for two years, living together for six months in a beautiful brownstone, which we had gutted down to the joists and joints. We picked out new cabinets, floors—everything—and Reece, who was working on his master's in interior design, redesigned it.

Our neighborhood was in an up-and-coming area of Washington, DC, called Eckington, with a very mixed population: straight and gay, white and black, old and young. There were some lingering gang activities, including a shooting in front of our home that Reece and I witnessed from our bedroom window. I had grown up in bad neighborhoods, places with bars on all the doors and windows, so I wasn't too affected by it, but Reece, who is from the Midwest and had only known nicer areas in DC, had been alarmed.

When Reece and I met, we both knew we wanted kids, but I'd always been adamant about adopting from overseas. I was ready to start right away; I was forty-two and had wanted a family for as long as I could remember. But Reece was insistent about finishing his master's first. In June, after Reece's graduation, we began planning in earnest.

That Saturday morning, we were flipping through the channels until we landed on a local program called *Wednesday's Child* with Barbara Harrison. It was a five-minute segment on the news they reran on Saturday mornings, which profiled a local child in the DC foster care system. The morning's episode was another heartbreaking story of a child whose parents had abused and neglected him, a child who was thrown into the system through no choice of his own. Before it was over, we were both wiping tears out of our eyes.

When the segment ended and the blare of commercials came on, Reece muted the TV and turned to me.

"Now," he said in that soft voice of his—direct but gentle— "explain to me again why we don't want to adopt locally?"

He was touching a finger to the stove. Reece didn't know every detail about my history yet, but he knew enough; he knew how much it weighed on me. He knew about my biological dad and stepfather and foster parents, things I carried from my past like heavy bags from place to place.

"I told you we would not talk about my past," I snapped, getting up to get more coffee. "I know what those kids are like."

"But, Rob," he said, following me to the kitchen, "you *were* one of those kids."

"Exactly, and I . . ." Just talking about *not* talking about it took superhuman strength. I didn't even want to turn around from the kitchen counter and face him. As though not looking at him meant I wouldn't have to discuss it anymore.

I had been telling myself a convenient story for many years. Not a lie, exactly—more like a cover. That story was that adopting overseas was both a quicker option and a way to avoid what I thought of as "the gay issue." But that wasn't really the complete truth, and Reece knew it. I probably knew it, too. There was a deeper reason I wouldn't even consider, one he drew out of me that morning. And he did it in that way that made me remember why I love him so much: not with force but with compassion.

I had been writing off these kids because I didn't want to address that part of my life. The last thing I wanted was to bring someone into my home who would every day remind me of my past. I refused to open that door.

"Do you realize the disservice you are doing to these kids by shutting that out? By shutting *them* out?" Reece said. "You're so worried about making sure what our friends think of you. But you haven't stopped to think about what those kids need."

I turned around, and I'm sure Reece could see that I had started to tear up.

"Rob," he said, stepping forward and taking my hand. "Remember the other night? That boy outside?"

Of course I did.

A few nights before, we had been jolted awake around 2:00 a.m. by a noise from one of our neighbors' houses. We looked out the window and were struck dumb to see a toddler playing in front on the sidewalk, the adults getting high and laughing on the porch. The whole scene just drove home what should have been so obvious.

I was being selfish, but until Reece brought it up, I hadn't seen it that way. It was a light bulb moment that opened something in me, but I was mad at him for making it happen. Why rock the boat now? For the first time, I was finally happy. We had great friends, lived comfortably, ate well, and drove nice cars. As someone who grew up extremely poor, these were not small things to me. Except for a child, I had everything I wanted.

But Reece didn't care if I had a brownstone or slept in my car. He didn't care if I had a PhD or was a high school dropout. He just loved me. This love felt like something I had wrapped around me at all times. Reece would be across the room and look at me and I could just feel it. And I'd never felt that certainty before, that *safety*. So part of me was mad at him for opening my eyes. But once they were open, I could see no other way.

"I failed them. I failed them," I said, crying. Reece put his arm around me and held me. The dam broke and it all just kept coming out. I had been so focused on what I had escaped from that I didn't think about all those who were still there. And what I could do about it.

•

Two days later, on a beautiful spring Monday morning, I took the day off from my job at the mortgage company. The easy light pushed through the windows as I got dressed, taking my breathing one inhale at a time. *We were starting.* Reece was working as a hairdresser at the time, with clients in the afternoon so, as on every step of this journey, we would go together.

We drove over to DC Child and Family Services, a cold and bureaucratic building downtown.

"This is it?" Reece said when we stepped inside the lobby.

"Well, what did you expect?"

He looked around—linoleum and tile and horrible fluorescent lights. "I don't know. Something homier. Warmer."

"Uh, no," I said as we searched for the right office. We found it, signed in, and waited on plastic chairs.

When it was our turn at the counter, I got straight to the point. I felt like I had been waiting forty-something years, so I wanted to get going. "We want to adopt a baby," I told the administrator. Even just saying the words felt like flipping a page in my life.

She was a stoic woman who eyed us up and down but said little.

On the drive over there, and in many conversations before, Reece had challenged me on this. Now he did it again. "Hang on a second, Rob. Why a baby?" he asked. "Are you going to be changing diapers?" He could just tell that I would be allergic to the whole idea of it, that my obsession with cleanliness and neatness wouldn't mesh with the down and dirty parts of babies.

I waved him off. "Oh, I'll get used to that," I said.

Reece playfully rolled his eyes. He knew he'd be the one diapering.

He gestured to me, and we took our conversation off to the side of the room.

"I want a baby," I said under my breath. "Then we don't have to worry about what it went through."

"But, Rob," Reece said, "that's who they were. That's who they are."

The conversation got cut off once the administrator there gave us a dose of reality: there was a two- to three-year waiting list to get a baby. I wasn't the only one who wanted a child without a past. No way I was going to wait that long—and even then, who knew what would happen? In fact, there was a long waiting list to adopt *any* child.

"But if you do foster-to-adopt," she said, "there's a good chance that you would get a child sooner. Much sooner."

"A baby?" I asked.

She shrugged. "*Could* be a baby."

A foster child. The idea again scratched at my own issues—of abandonment, of separation, of the unknown. I was reluctant to bring in a foster child, too, because when the child ultimately reunited with the family, the loss would break me into pieces.

But we had come this far. She gave us a schedule of the orientation classes, handed us a pamphlet about foster parenting, and we went home. That night over Rachael Ray's Lazy Bolognese-Style Lasagna, which I had just learned to make, we continued the conversation.

I set up our TV tray tables in the living room. "You know," I said to Reece, "a foster child probably won't stay here for very long. They're going to go back to their mom's or their dad's. That's what happens to foster children. Trust me—"

"I know, Rob. But that doesn't matter," Reece said. "If we can change a child's life, even for a day, don't you feel like we should do that? What if somebody would've done that for you?"

I had absolutely no response. He was right again. That's the thing about Reece—he's always right. More than just the voice of reason in our home, Reece spoke to what I knew in my heart was true but was often too hurt or selfish or scared to admit. Reece is the smartest person I know; he always looks at the big picture. I tend to zero in on the problem at hand. And I miss so many things that way.

Since we first agreed to adopt, I had just been thinking about me—how it would affect me, how it would remind me of bad memories. Reece kept forcing me to step outside myself. My attachment issues ran deep, and this journey was going to be hard for me no matter how we moved forward. I could not shut out those feelings. It seemed I would never shake the fear of being left behind, which hovered over every close relationship I ever had. It followed me around like an ominous cloud.

After talking about it some more, we agreed that we'd take a child under the age of five. Every step along the way, Reece turned me forward. When we were filling out the forms, I kept angling for the perfect child, and Reece kept shutting that down. "As a parent you don't get to decide whether your child is blind," he said. "You don't get to decide if your child is deaf. You don't get to decide whether that child has any handicap."

"Yeah, but—"

"We are not getting a designer child, Rob."

The way Reece said it made me ashamed about being picky. It was obvious: we'd take any child who needed a home. We made plans to begin orientation in a couple of weeks and that was that. We were two city guys—madly in love—embarking on a journey that we thought we knew something about. But we had no idea.

2

WHAT I REMEMBER

I am three years old. It's the middle of the night, and I'm sleeping on a big, hard mattress with my sisters in a hot room, wearing just a diaper. I'm being lightly shaken—once, twice—and then I'm awake. My eyes adjust to my mother's face hovering over me. She puts a finger over her lips. "*Shhhh.*"

My big sisters, Fran and Beth, aren't in the bed next to me. They are standing in their pajamas by the rectangle light of the door frame. Mom is wearing a ragged nightgown, old-fashioned and once white. "Terry," she whispers. My first name is Robert, but everyone calls me by my middle name.

Fran comes forward and picks me up in her arms. And we go.

We all quietly begin to walk down the creaky stairs. The moldy and musty smell covers everything. Then we're all tiptoeing out the door and down the two concrete steps to the yard.

Hitting the fresh air, we all run behind the house, through the backyard, and into a nearby field, where we crouch down in the tall grass. Behind us, up the hill, I can see the train tracks. For fun, we sometimes roll big brown barrels down that hill. Fran warns me all the time never to walk on those tracks. It is too dangerous.

No one warns me about the danger inside our house.

"Frances!" The sound of my dad's ragged voice calling my mother cuts the muggy night like a thunder crack. "Frances! Frances May!" His voice is deep and angry, worn harsh and mean by decades of smoking and drinking, the sound of something ugly and dark.

I hold on to Fran's shoulders, petrified, and shake at the sound of his screaming. Fran holds me tight. After the yelling stops for a bit, she puts me on my belly down in the grass. When I try to stand, she gently pushes me down.

The four of us stay out there for hours. No sounds but my dad's voice, the chirp of crickets, and the occasional roar of the train in the thick night.

"Where the fuck are you?! Frances May! Get the fuck back in this house!"

Mom stays quiet. It's summertime and there are mosquitos in the muggy air, but it's safer out here. She's putting it off as long as she can, but once Dad finds her, he is just going to beat her up or hit all of us. Everyone knows how this is going to end.

Once the screams go silent for long enough, my mother knows he's asleep.

We sneak back into the house to find him passed out on the

couch, his prematurely white hair mussed and a loud snore bellow-
ing from his nose. Dad is in nothing but a pair of old boxer shorts.
He wears them all the time, no matter who is around, always making sure people can see everything. This is who he is, wearing his
ugliness front and center, out for all to see.

I think about that night a lot—the pain and the fear, the
uncertainty—but there is also my mother's and sisters' love and
impulse to protect: two sides of the same coin. Abuse and affection
tied together. It would take more than thirty years for me to learn
to separate the two.

•

My parents are having one of their shared drunken, drug-fueled
rages. My father, beer and cigarettes wafting off him, has lined
Fran, Beth, and me up in a row. We are kneeling on the kitchen
floor right in front of the white refrigerator. It's an ugly and dingy
kitchen—dirty dishes piled up, filled ashtrays on the tabletops, a
layer of grime on everything.

My father is holding his gun, taking turns pointing the shiny
metal at each of our heads.

He and my mother are laughing.

"They're scared, Frances!" he yells over to my mom. "They're
pissing themselves they're so scared."

We *are* scared. I look over at Fran, the oldest, who usually takes things in stride, and even she looks scared. She's staring straight ahead, her lips a straight line.

I don't hear what my mother says, but I hear the laugh in her voice. The drinks are slurring her words and clouding any last bit of good sense she might have.

"Which one do you want me to shoot first?" my father asks her.

We're all silent; the loud hum of the refrigerator is the only sound. My knees are starting to hurt. I want to squirm, change my position, but I don't want to set my father off.

He reaches on top of the refrigerator for what I think are bullets. He takes some out of a white box and tries to shove them into the gun. He's so drunk he drops a few, picks them up from the floor, tries again to jam them into the gun, muttering to himself. He's sloppy and dangerous and terrifying. I hear the sound of something snapping shut. He looks over to me and points the gun right at my head. He pauses for an extra few seconds, and I close my eyes.

He pulls the trigger. *Click*. Silence. The click sends a cold current through my whole body.

Sometimes, when things are dark, I feel that shiver again.

•

There is yelling behind my parents' closed bedroom door. My mother walks out, and I see one eye swollen shut. Her face is a mask. She is quiet and stoic, and I don't know what she is thinking.

Sometimes she takes the beatings to protect us. But she's human and worn down, so she gets tired of it. There are rages she doesn't feel like bearing, so she lets him beat us.

Sometimes she lets him do other things.

•

I'm in the kitchen with my sister Beth. "Terry!" I hear my father yell from the living room. He wants me to get him a beer from the refrigerator. I either don't hear him the first time he asks or am not fast enough, so he gets angrier.

"Get your ass in here!"

When I get close to him, in comes that smell, *God*, that nauseating smell like a heavy presence around him. He brings me closer and puts the lit part of his cigarette into the bare flesh of my leg, the cherry burning my skin. There's a brief sizzling sound, and it hurts so much I want to scream. He has done this a few times, sometimes for no reason. But even the reasons aren't reasons.

•

I am five years old on my way to bed. As I pass in front of my parents' door, I see it is cracked open. I peer in, like peeking at a movie I'm not supposed to watch. My mom is on the floor crying, wailing. My father is screaming, pointing a gun at her head.

I think this is what families do. Everyone who comes around is just like them. How am I to know any different?

•

Mom is usually quiet and reserved, though with a couple of drinks in her she comes to life. Alcohol smothers whatever fear she usually hides. She has hazel eyes like mine, behind cat-eyed glasses, and a soft face. Her smile is lopsided but perfect. I think she is the most beautiful woman in the world.

At night I watch her tease her hair up with hair spray, twirl it in soft curlers. She wraps it in toilet paper before she goes to bed, a long Salem cigarette burning a trail of smoke in the ashtray. I watch it wisp upward in curlicues.

My mother is like a gypsy; there's just no other word for it. We are constantly living here, moving there, leaving my dad, going back to my dad, staying with this man, leaving that man. We have so many uncles—who I later learn are boyfriends and ex-husbands. Fran, Beth, and I all have different fathers.

All told, my mother will be married seven times and bear ten children.

I can't imagine what her life was like before all of us. She is like a blank slate, reemerging each time with a new man and new children, hitting reset on her life so many times she doesn't know which one she's living.

Fran is eight years older than me, not yet a teenager, but more like a mother than our mom is. Fran makes sure Beth and I are always fed and dressed. She barely goes to school because she takes care of me.

We move around so much and those houses and rooms all blend together; there's nothing linking one with the next. No friends, no teachers who know us, nothing sturdy to build a childhood on. There is not a thing in any house that makes it feel like a home. We are always one box away from having to move—nothing on the walls, temporary furniture covered in dust.

We might as well have picked up the same empty, lifeless house and moved it around Virginia, Maryland, and North Carolina. No turkey dinner for Thanksgiving, no present or tree for Christmas, no basket of chocolate for Easter. Nothing. I never even have a birthday party. We live in so many different places that I don't start school until first grade.

After my father breaks her arm, my mother leaves us all for a while. While she's gone Dad has sex with the neighbor woman in front of Fran, Beth, and me. We are right there on the couch. I don't know if he doesn't realize we are there or if he likes it. We don't ask.

Our lives are a steady series of unsteadiness. Mom leaves Dad a few times, sometimes leaving us with him, sometimes taking us with her. We live with an earlier husband of hers and her children from that marriage. Another time Mom's brother and his wife, and their twelve children, take us in, an appendage to another family.

My sisters and I are constantly going back and forth to my uncle and aunt's house, to the shelter, to my dad's house, back to my mom's boyfriend's house, back to a babysitter's house, back to my aunt and uncle's house. That's what life always is—floating.

•

We go to church on Sundays—Southern Baptist—where old women wear hats and people lose control of their bodies. Sometimes they say made-up words, speak in tongues. Like they are taken over by the Holy Spirit.

Dad plays his holier-than-thou routine in his tucked dress shirt and jeans, his ears sticking out from his neatly slicked hair. People call him "Mr. Chasteen" and he acts like an upstanding member of the community, but we're never fooled. He brings along his mother, the meanest woman alive. Her stern face never breaks. Though he beats us over and over again, like a Sunday ritual, right in front of her, she never says a thing.

My father goes through phases in which he finds religion. Or pretends to. He puts them on sometimes like a new hat, but it always feels fake. Sometimes Dad forces us to go to these big tent revivals that come to town. He makes some money helping to raise the tent and set up the service.

Under the tent, I sit, wearing shoes that don't fit and hand-me-down clothes. The preacher pulls out a snake, and I'm scared so I look away. I see my dad walking down the aisle with an offering tray, collecting money for the church. Or that's what he's supposed to be doing.

•

At some point both of my parents are working in the same cotton mill but different shifts. Dad works days so we are home with him alone at night. That's when he takes me into his room. It happens mostly when Mom is out of the house, but she knows. She is there sometimes.

My father is in the shower. I hear the water running through the thin walls of the house and my stomach clenches like a fist. Then I hear him yell, "Frances! Frances, bring Robert Terry in here!" I start crying. I know what's going to happen.

My mother grabs me and shakes me. "Just stop crying, Terry," she says. "Just stop crying." She walks me into the bathroom. Steam fills up the room, and my father whips the shower curtain open and brings me in. She leaves and shuts the door behind her.

•

I am a scared little kid, so I pee in my pants all the time. Every time, my father beats me even worse for it. He uses his belts, but also his fists, punching me in my gut, hitting me in my groin. He makes me hold in my pee; I do it for so many years that one day, when I am older, my bladder will rupture.

There is abuse and then there are the emotional scars beyond abuse. I am so terrified and confused that being molested by my father isn't even the worst thing to me. Everything is backward, but I don't know this. At least he is giving me attention. *How can he love me unless he hurts me?*

This is the only type of family that I know. I don't know why my mother had us at all. We always feel like we are a burden. We *are* a burden—there is no other way to feel.

· 3 ·

COMING BACK

July 2008

On a muggy Saturday morning, Reece and I traveled out to DC Child and Family Services for our first orientation meeting to be foster parents. We were both anxious—I was talking too much, as I tend to do from nerves, while fiddling with the radio and the windows. Reece usually does the opposite when he's nervous, so he was quiet. When we walked in, we noticed we were the only gay couple there, but that wasn't an issue for me. The problem was the memories, and the second we walked in, they came back ferociously.

That whole morning was a flashback of the system and everything I knew about it. In an overly air-conditioned conference room, prospective parents crowded around the instructor before we even began. And it had nothing to do with giving homes to needy kids.

"When do we get our check?"

"How much is the check?"

"If we get a bigger house, can we get more kids and a bigger check?"

It seemed that every discussion went back to what was in it for them. I stayed silent, but I was fuming the whole time.

Four hours later, when it was over, I was enraged. On our way out the door, before we even hit the parking lot, I told Reece, "There's no fucking way I'm coming back here."

"Yes we are, Rob," he said, calm but defiant. "Every Saturday until we've completed it."

"Wait a second," I said. "Were you not just in there with me? Did you not see what just happened in there?"

"I was there."

"Those people could not give a damn about any kids, Reece. They just wanted to get paid."

"Well, that's all the more reason—"

"Sorry, I just can't," I said, getting into the car. "I can't. Let's do the overseas route. Let's start that up again."

"Rob, take a breath. Just breathe. It's not about that. It's about the difference we can make in a child's life. We're not giving up."

"It's too hard, Reece. It's just . . ." I said.

"Think about when you were a kid. What if someone had invested in you? Everything you say is *more* reason we need to be doing this."

Reece is an optimist, but he is also forceful when necessary. He said exactly what I needed to hear at that moment, while I was still having trouble untangling my own experience as a child from what we were going through. Reece was there to keep me grounded.

The following Saturday, the room was weeded down to maybe fifteen people, each of whom was a bit more committed than the previous week. We all sat at a big conference room table and for eight straight Saturdays learned what DC thought a parent should be.

A few sessions in, the instructor was going over foster care rules and procedures when all of a sudden we heard a snap, the sound of a metal can opening. We all looked over, and at the end of the table, a man had opened a beer.

"Uh, you know, you can't have that here," the instructor said.

"Why not?" he asked, taking a big sip. "This is what I do on Saturday. And this is taking up my Saturday."

"No, we're not having a beer," she said, somehow less surprised than I thought she should be. "This is neither the time nor the place."

He placed the beer back in the cooler and grumbled under his breath. Reece and I met eyes. He was shocked, but I was not. It was revolting but par for the course.

During another class, we were talking about proper discipline and what boundaries were important.

"Every once in a while," one man said, "the only thing that'll get through to these kids is a good ass whipping."

A few others nodded and chimed in their yeses, like it was the most obvious parenting philosophy in the world.

These people should not be parents, I thought. Every father, every older man in my life had hurt me. That was how every conflict had been handled in every house I'd grown up in. When I started to raise my hand like I was going to respond, and furiously, Reece put his hand over mine. I stayed silent, letting my feelings stew.

Sitting there, listening to how this cycle was just going to continue, drove home to me the problem with the system. It's not about quality care—it's about beds. That's the ball game. The more beds the state and the county get, the more money they get. Period. Because of that, they have to keep the floodgates open. Outside of having a criminal record, nothing will get you rejected as a foster parent. The economics of the state is dependent on it. The states need to keep the number of kids in care up because that keeps the federal money rolling in. It's a system of self-interest.

Those classes were brutal, and I bit my tongue constantly, but it reinforced what Reece already knew: we were doing the right thing. Kids out there needed people like us giving them a home—if only so they wouldn't go to one of these other homes.

We wanted to be parents so badly that within two months we had already finished everything they needed from us. We had to get complete physicals, our finances checked, CPR certification, our home inspected by a fire marshal and tested for lead paint. They also checked us for HIV, something no other foster parents I spoke to had to be tested for.

We were so under the microscope during all this that Reece and

I didn't even question the HIV testing. I had come out of the closet in the 1980s, when that kind of discrimination was common. In 2008, gay people were still not allowed to give blood, and I was used to people not sharing a bottle with me. That was the behavior I knew and I certainly wasn't going to rock the boat by complaining.

Once we completed our orientation, there was not a single piece of additional paperwork we needed to complete. The rooms at our home were all set up: a baby's room and a toddler's room—because we didn't know the age we were going to get—both filled with toys.

Everything in our lives was ready for that call to happen. So Reece and I waited to receive a placement.

And we waited.

And waited.

•

By September we had everything approved. October unfolded into November. Not a word. December at our home was quiet and devastating. When I was growing up, holidays were never acknowledged, much less celebrated. Since getting together with Reece, I had embraced the holiday spirit, so my expectations for that Christmas were vivid: we'd be watching a child opening presents under our Christmas tree. That was a picture I played in my mind over and over again: baking cookies, singing carols, decorating the house. But that Christmas ended up feeling like a slap in the face, a reminder of what we didn't have. The upstairs rooms remained empty and the longer we waited, the more the whole house started to feel empty.

Every week, dumfounded and enraged, I phoned DC Child and Family Services. I had educated myself on the number of kids flooding into the DC foster care system. What became clear over time was that the woman in charge was not interested in giving a child to two white gay men. Every other parent from our orientation class had already been given a kid by this point; we were the only ones left waiting. Reece has always been trusting, willing to give people the benefit of the doubt, so it took some time for him to see it. But eventually the evidence was overwhelming: they just didn't want us to have a child.

When we had finished orientation, we wanted to make sure the city knew we took the process seriously. That a child could walk into our house and not want for a thing. The home study assessor told us she had never seen parents so well prepared for a child to enter their home. We were not being picky about what kind of child we brought in. We just wanted to be foster parents.

Meanwhile we saw what other foster parents in orientation class were like; the fact that they were getting kids before us made me sick to my stomach. This dreadful wait was the first time—but not the last—that we dealt with people, agencies, and institutions who felt that Reece and I shouldn't have children in our lives.

"It's never gonna happen," I said to Reece one night, in tears. "It's just never gonna happen."

"It'll happen. Just let it play out," he said.

"It doesn't make any sense. How can this be? It's been five months."

I was close to giving up, but Reece held out hope, assuring me that these things take time and we'd get a call soon. And I had no choice but to believe him.

•

During the first week of the new year, I called DC Child and Family Services again, at that point just going through the motions. My hope had been sapped, and merely making the call was a punishing process. Then a new voice answered the phone.

"Hi," I said, thrown off. "Does Diana still work there?"

"No, she's been transferred somewhere else. This is Cheryl. How may I help you?"

"Oh, well, my name is Rob Chasteen. We've had our application in since last summer to be foster parents, and you know, I've probably been everybody's thorn, but I'm calling again to get a placement."

"Hold on a sec." She was gone for a few minutes. When she came back on the line, she apologized. "Mr. Chasteen, I am so sorry. Your application has been at the bottom of the pile."

"You're kidding."

"No, honey, I wish I were. I don't know why this has been passed over."

But it was no mystery to me. We were lucky—the new woman didn't care who we were, just that we were prepared and that we wanted to be parents. She was thinking about the well-being of the children, which is the *only* thing she should have been thinking about. It seemed like no one else had been.

A week later, my phone rang at work, and it was Cheryl again.

"Mr. Chasteen, I have some news," she said, her voice giving away what it was.

My heart went into my throat. I'd been waiting for this call for six months. "I got your application here," she said, "and I know you said you only wanted one child, but I have a brother and a sister and I just think they'd be an amazing fit for you two."

Reece and I had recently talked about siblings. "If for any reason there are siblings," he'd said, "we're not going to ever split them up." I'd agreed.

So I already knew where Reece stood, but I called him to be sure.

"Two?" he said, audibly taken aback.

"Yeah," I said, "but we're not gonna split them up."

"No, of course not," he said. I could hear hesitance in his voice.

"Remember what you said about parents not getting to choose who or what their kids were?"

"Yes," he said. "Of course."

"Well, this is that," I said. "There are two kids. That's what there is."

"You're right," Reece said. "Okay, let's meet them."

I called Cheryl back.

"We're open to siblings," I said. "When could we all meet?"

"How's tonight at seven o'clock?" she asked. Her question crashed over me like a wave. My hopes for the future and my dream of a family swept through me. But there was more that flooded in: the suddenness of change, the unsteady ground that defined my childhood.

"Tonight?"

4

ONE WITH ANOTHER

I am six years old and haven't seen my mother for three months. None of us have. Fran, Beth, and I are all living at my dad's in North Carolina, and we don't know where she is. Our father tells us he's tired of us. He hasn't heard from Mom and he's going to send us to an orphanage. He isn't going to deal with us anymore.

Fran is inside, packing all our stuff.

Beth is still at school.

I am playing in the front yard.

Then a rusted blue station wagon pulls into the driveway. I see my mother behind the wheel, her beehive hairdo touching the roof. She waves me over. When I get to the car, I see Beth in the back seat. I am scared because I don't know what's going on. My father is awful, but he never changes. Even the orphanage threat doesn't feel real. Mom comes in and out of our lives without ever explaining herself, especially to me. I don't know what to think of this, that she's just pulled up into our driveway.

"Where's Fran?" Mom asks.

"Inside," I say.

"Get her to come outside."

"Okay." I turn to go into the house.

"Terry!" she whisper yells.

"Yeah?"

"Don't say I'm here. Just get her outside."

I run in and see my dad sitting in his chair with his cigarette, smoke rising up around him.

Fran looks up when I walk in. "Come here," I say. "I wanna show you something."

"Terry, I gotta get this done." She gestures to the packing.

"You gotta come outside."

"What? Why?"

"You have to come outside," I say. My dad's eyes are still on the TV.

Fran finally follows me out the front door. "What? Terry, what?" Then she looks over and sees my mom. The two of them talk at the car window, but I can't hear them. Then Fran gets in the front seat, and they tell me to get in the back with Beth.

My mom pulls out of the driveway and takes off.

We literally have just the clothes on our backs, leaving every-thing behind. Our belongings weren't much, but they were all we had. Now we have nothing.

It's quiet for a while in the car. We are on the highway, cars speeding past, and no one says a word. Finally, Fran—always Fran—speaks up. "Where are we going?"

Silence from my mother. Her right hand stays on the wheel, eyes glued to the road. Her other hand nervously flicks ash out the window. I know better than to ask questions, but my fear hasn't lifted. It just feels like another left turn in a life that is full of them. It is a roller coaster that never lets us relax.

"Mom?"

She takes a big breath. "Yes, Fran."

"Where are we going?"

"Uncle Bruce's."

Uncle Bruce lives in Maryland; I don't know how far that is, but I know it's a whole other place. I know his sons touch me when I don't want them to. I know better than to tell anyone about it.

There is a hole in the floor of the station wagon and I watch the blacktop whip by under my feet.

My mom doesn't ask what happened while she was gone and never gives a reason for leaving us. The only thing she ever says is she had been "trying to make a life for all of us." I don't understand this. Every time she leaves, our life is worse. *How is this making anything?*

Next to me in the back, Beth is crying. She's been crying for most of the ride. When my mother snaps and tells her to stop, Beth says she wants to go back and get her favorite shoes. "We're not turning around," my mother says very matter-of-factly. It's not up for discussion.

I don't say a word. I don't care if we go or if we stay. I just want my mother to meet my eyes in that mirror, tell me she loves me, that everything is going to be okay. In some ways, Mom hurts me more than Dad because she brings me in and then pushes me away, lifting my hopes up only to drop them. Fran and Beth have learned to go with the flow, but I never have.

Mom smokes long Salem Lights, pulling one out of the green pack every few minutes and lighting it. Old country plays on the radio, tough women going through hard times, like Loretta Lynn and Patsy Cline. Mom has a beautiful voice, and she and Fran sing along in the front seat. *Crazy . . . crazy for feeling so lonely.*

I stare at the floor and watch the road whoosh by.

I will never see my dad again and I will never miss him, not for a single second.

•

Uncle Bruce and Aunt Tara have twelve kids. We don't stay with them for long and end up moving in with my mother's sister, Aunt Mary. My mom works at a Chinese restaurant as a waitress—she brings leftovers home in plain white boxes all the time. That's all we eat, cold Chinese food out of cartons, which I get used to. For a while, I like our life, mostly just glad my dad is far, far away, and Mom never mentions his name.

Uncle Bruce and Aunt Tara own a strip club across the border in Virginia. It's a dark and loud place where topless women dance in front of poles on raised platforms. My mom is there all the time with Bruce and Tara, so we are there all the time. Fran, Beth, and I are always sitting in the back room, where the women change into their pasties and G-strings.

There is a dancer there we call Aunt Suge, who babysits us along with my cousins. Suge is a large woman with really short platinum-blond hair. Her boobs are so big she can use them to lift and pour a pitcher of beer, a trick us kids love. She is gentle and sweet and often wraps her big arms around me in a hug. Even though it's a little gross, all her flabby skin flopping down, her hugs make me feel good.

One time my mother is out drinking with Uncle Bruce and Aunt Tara, and Suge is watching all of us, including the cousins. When the adults get home, Suge tells them we were misbehaving—somebody had been trying to climb out the window. My aunt ties three extension cords together and lines us all up. She and my uncle proceed to whip us on our backs and legs. I am the youngest so I'm relieved that by the time they get to me, they're exhausted. I only get hit once, and it's not so bad.

•

My mom takes a job at a Catholic nursing home and has to hide that we exist because it'll be easier for her. One day she tells us we are going to live during the week at a stranger's house she found in an advertisement, a woman named Shelly. Shelly is a big, mean woman with two daughters and a husband I rarely see. For most of the day, it is a house full of girls—Shelly, her two daughters, and my two sisters.

Shelly is just a flat-out scary person so I try to stay out of her way. This is not always possible. I call underwear "panties" because that's what everyone else in the house calls them. "They're not panties!" Shelly yells at me. "Panties are for girls!"

Soon after, she takes me into the woods down the block, puts a pair of panties on me, and makes me walk home like that.

Her husband sleeps on the floor next to me and touches me in the middle of the night. I don't make a sound. Shelly knows—but she says nothing. She does nothing.

Once, my sisters and Shelly's daughters all skip school, and she is furious. She locks my sisters out of the house and I stand in the living room at the glass door looking out at them, crying hysterically. "Stop crying!" she screams at me. Then she takes a belt and starts beating me with it. Shelly's temper is like a fire. Once she gets in one of her rages, she cannot stop. It just takes her over.

One time we go over to Aunt Mary's for a weekend to see my mother and I am completely covered, dressed from head to toe. It is the middle of the summer. "Why is he dressed like that?" my mother asks Fran.

"You need to go into the bedroom. Go and look at him," Fran says. "Take his clothes off."

Fran, my mother, and Aunt Mary take me to the bedroom and start to remove my clothes. I wince as they take down my pants and look: I am covered from neck to feet in bruises where Shelly had beaten me with the belt strap and the buckle. My groin area, my legs, my stomach, my back. Purple and black and blue.

My mother is furious—but not because I am hurt.

"What am I supposed to do on Monday for work? I can't take him back to Shelly's house now!" my mother screams. "Where do I put him?!" She has no choice but to leave the job. I take the blame.

•

One night a man comes into my aunt and uncle's strip club in his green electrician's uniform. He's a big man who looks like John Wayne with a bit of an Elvis sneer. He smokes Winstons and has really bad teeth. He's always squeezing oil into his hands from this bottle he carries around in his pocket and rubbing the oil into his hair. Then he takes out his black comb and combs a perfect part, like he's in an old movie. One day, Mom sits my sisters and me down on the couch and introduces him to us.

"This will be your new dad," she says. His name is Frank.

Frank is a yeller, a big and sturdy man with a booming voice. After they get married, we move to a new apartment. It's a strange place, and I am scared. I watch Frank take my mother into the bedroom and lock the door. Outside their door, I sit, banging on it and crying, "Mom, Mom!" Soon Frank opens up the door, picks me up, and slams me down on the kitchen counter.

"Hey! Hey, you little shit! Stop it!" he yells, right up in my face. I can see his yellow and crooked teeth. "You will never be like this in my fucking family!" Then he slaps me hard across the face. "If I ever hear you cry like that again, I'll give you something twice as bad."

The next day, my mother doesn't mention it. To her, it is like it never happened.

Frank is just as abusive to me as my dad was, if not more so. I do what I can to not make him angry, but he's unpredictable. He smacks me for no reason. He always grabs my mother's arm with such force that the color drains out of it. I see the grimace on her face, the flinch of her body.

Frank has an obsession about things being clean and puts the fear of God into us about it. Our house is immaculate, but we are always on edge about cleaning up every little thing. We are put on restriction for even the smallest mistake, like not capping the toothpaste. Once, when I don't clean underneath my bed, Frank puts me on restriction for most of the summer. I spend two months in my room, only allowed out to eat dinner. It's like prison. But I know better than to ever complain.

●

Mom has no belly button. When I was younger, she showed me the large scar across her stomach, saying it was from a surgery she had before I was born. She had gone to the hospital to get the cancer removed and that's when she found out she was pregnant with me. I was unexpected—the last of her ten children. She went in with cancer and came out with me.

When I am nine, my mother gets cancer again—a different kind—and doctors have to remove one of her breasts. She comes home from the hospital and calls me to the bedroom. When I am in there, she asks me to come close. I hesitate, a little wary.

"Come here, Terry," she says. I walk slowly toward her.

She sits up in bed and opens up her pink satin pajamas. There's this bandage across her chest. She takes it off and shows me a gigantic scar.

"The cancer is gone now, Terry. I'm going to be okay."

I put my head on her shoulder, loving the feel of those soft pajamas on my face. I close my eyes, and am safe.

●

It is Wednesday night, Mom's bingo night. It's the part of the week I always dread because once she leaves, Frank gets drunk and finds a reason to punish us or beat us with a belt. I beg her not to go, but she's not listening. She's busy fixing dinner. While she's in the kitchen, I sneak upstairs to her bedroom. On the dresser, I find the silicone breast she tucks into her bra when she goes out. I grab a bobby pin from the makeup table, open its jaws, and drive it through the fake breast. The silicone oozes out. When Mom comes up and finds it, she starts screaming at me. "Robert Terry, what's wrong with you?! Why did you do that? I can't go out without this!"

Of course I know this. I get such a beating, but I don't care. Anything so she won't leave.

•

On Thanksgiving, we all pile into the Chrysler and drive down to Florida to meet Frank's brother, the first we've ever heard of Frank's family. I don't think of Frank as even having a family. He doesn't seem like someone who would.

On the way there, my sister Fran gets her first period, bleeding onto the white interior of the car's back seat. On the highway, Frank pulls the car over and screams all hell at Fran. He gets into the back and tries to clean the seat, alternating between muttering to himself and yelling at Fran. I watch as my mother and Fran walk away from the car and talk. I don't understand the blood, but Mom doesn't seem alarmed. Frank just stews for the rest of the trip and we all stay silent in the back seat.

Fran is a teenager now and she runs away a few times, once to be a go-go dancer, another time to join a carnival. When she is fifteen, she leaves for the last time. She tells Frank and my mom she is pregnant and needs their permission to get married. I find out later the pregnancy was a lie; she just wanted out of there. She is the closest thing to a real mother that I've ever known, and I can't shake the emptiness when she's gone. I cry for days, like a part of my body has been ripped off.

Fran marries a much older man who treats her terribly and beats her up. She ends up living my mother's story, her same bad choices. One day, so will Beth. And so will I.

•

When I am eleven, Mom's cancer comes back like it's angry. One day she just up and leaves, and Beth tells me she is living with Uncle Bruce and Aunt Tara. Once in a while Frank drives us out there for a short visit with Mom, where we sit on a couch with this person I don't even recognize. It's all very confusing. Mom is this emaciated stranger with a white turban hiding her bald head, too weak to move much or talk very loud. I am so happy to see her, even this version of her, even for just an hour, that I usually cry when we get home.

Beth and I are at home alone one night watching a TV movie about ice-skaters on the floor of the basement. It's an old TV, one where we have to get up to turn the knob to change the channel, a silver antenna poking out of the top.

I hear Frank walk in and so I stare at the ceiling. I hope he doesn't come down the stairs, hope he just goes to bed and sleeps off whatever is making him angry. Then there's the sound of his boots coming down the creaking steps. Slower than normal. A heavy walk.

We don't look at him. I keep my eyes on the screen, watching Jimmy McNichol.

"Just want to let you know your mom died," he says. "We'll figure out the funeral."

Beth and I don't move. We don't say a word.

"I don't know if you guys are hungry," he says. "Hopefully you ate."

Then he goes back upstairs.

5

A NEW KIND OF EMPTY

January 2009

"Hello? Mr. Chasteen? Are you there?"

Her question pulls me from my reverie. I hadn't realized I'd gone silent. I was staring out my window at work and had spaced out for a moment. "Yes," I said. "I'm sorry. I'm here."

"I asked if you and Reece are free to meet the kids tonight," Cheryl said. Months of waiting for a call and now this. The speed of light. My stomach dropped. "I can have the social worker there with them at seven o'clock."

"Yes. Sure. Thank you." I was already looking around the office to gauge how quickly I could get out of there. My voice was calm, but the blood started rushing through my body and the details flooded my brain: *Is the house ready? Are all sharp things put away? Do we have enough toys? Is there time to go buy more?*

I hung up and immediately called Reece.

"I just talked to Child and Family Services," I said, my words running together, my breath tight. "They want us to meet the kids tonight. What should I do?"

"Well, first, you should just breathe," he said. Reece never got overwhelmed; I usually panicked enough for both of us. "Just hang out until I get there. It'll be fine."

•

A few hours later I was home, getting the brownstone ready, spinning what-ifs through my mind until I made myself sick. I'm slightly obsessive about my home; it probably comes from growing up in a series of anonymous cold and empty houses. Not a single one of those places was a home, so it was important to me that Reece and I lived in a place that felt like a home. It mattered to me that the children, when they arrived, felt like they had walked into one.

Social workers had already been in and out of our house for months inspecting it, so I knew it was officially ready for kids. But it didn't *feel* kid friendly. It was a place decorated for what we were: two childless gay men who liked to entertain guests. Most of it was more museum than playroom. To give it a cozier feel, Reece had bought bigger pillows and draped blankets over the couches. But he is an interior designer, and we owned a nude male statue and charcoal paintings of men, all of which I hid in the closet before the social worker and children showed up. After dealing with so much homophobia just to get to this point, we didn't want one little thing to take it all away. Any object that might read as "gay" to someone who just walked in I put out of sight.

I rearranged items, took a look, and then moved them all back to their original spots. The neighbors kept Bailey for a few hours, since I was too worried that he would accidentally hurt one of the kids. I put cereal puffs in a container out on the counter, a bowl of fruit in the center of the dining room table. *But could the kids reach that?* I wondered. *I guess I'll probably just get it for them.* I scooped up a handful of toys and baskets from the two child bedrooms and brought them down to the living room: giant Lego blocks, a baby doll, a basket of stuffed animals, Dora the Explorer and Wonder Pets toys. Reece and I hadn't been idle during those months waiting for a call. We had devoured Nickelodeon shows, got CDs for the car to learn every kid song.

I was on the phone with Reece the entire time freaking out: "What if she doesn't like us? What if they don't like us?"

"Just be yourself," he said. "Remember what *they're* feeling. They're probably as scared and nervous as you are. You'll be great. I'll be there soon. I love you."

•

At 7:00 p.m. exactly, the doorbell rang. Even though I had been checking the clock relentlessly, the buzz still startled me; I had been locked inside my head for hours. I opened the door to find Sheri, the social worker, holding a little boy with long cornrows and big, black eyes. He was two but he looked really little, less than a year old. Holding Sheri's hand was a young girl, her hair done in plats and lots of barrettes, every single one a different bright color. The pop of color was such a contrast to her face, which was stoic. Defeated, even.

"This is Maya," Sheri said. "Maya, say hi to Mr. Rob. And this is Makai." Makai didn't react.

"Hi, Makai. Hi, Maya." I bent down to her level. "I'm Rob." Maya's big, brown eyes looked at me. I noticed a cute big space between her front teeth.

"Hi," Maya said, averting her gaze. She had the saddest face in the world. There was simply no other way to describe it.

"Please come in," I said.

When they all walked in, Maya immediately went for the large, green concrete horse in our living room—a piece of art that sat next to the table on a chest. She climbed up to sit on it. "Maya, you can't sit on that," Sheri snapped.

"No, no, it's fine. She can," I said. "We have a rule in the house— if it's here, everybody can touch it."

"Well, okay," Sheri said, easing a bit. "The last house they were in, they broke some of the woman's art, and she was *not* happy."

"There's nothing we have that would upset us if the kids broke it," I said. "If that were the case, we'd put it away."

"Okay. Good," Sheri said, making her way to the living room. She placed Makai on the white rug next to the coffee table, which was padded. Maya sat down on the couch, and I sat with her, close but giving her space.

There was a long pause—as the kids got adjusted, as Sheri waited for me to lead, as I tried to carefully navigate one of the biggest moments of my life.

I exhaled, trying to shut out my anxiety. To get some momentum, I just started asking questions. "So, Maya, how old are you now?" She held up four fingers without a smile, not even a little one. Just matter-of-factly. I had never seen a little kid so resigned, and my heart just sank.

"Wow," I said. "You're getting big."

Sheri passed through to the open dining room and sat on one of the chairs, watching us from a short distance.

"Anyone hungry?" I asked. "Are you hungry, Maya?" She immediately nodded her head, and I went to the kitchen and brought her the container of puffs. I gestured that she could go through the basket of toys and then spread some blocks in front of Makai. He just sat there on the floor, his eyes so empty.

I didn't say much to Sheri, trying to pay attention to the kids. But once she got going, she talked nonstop, mostly about how much trouble Makai was and how wiped out she was. I didn't want to be rude—this woman's opinion of us would hold enormous sway—but I was more focused on the kids.

I picked up different toys and dolls, trying to engage Maya, to make her feel comfortable. I thought about what Reece had said—*remember what they're feeling*. And I knew adults could be scary, especially new ones in a strange home.

"You're in preschool?" I asked.

Maya nodded.

"How do you like it?"

She shook her head. "I don't," she said, not really looking up. She grabbed a stuffed dog from the table.

"Oh, no? That's too bad," I said. "I loved school. My partner, Reece, who'll be here soon, loved it so much he went for thirty years." I smiled. "Maybe as you get older you'll like it."

She just shrugged.

"Do you have a favorite color?" I asked.

She nodded. A silent beat passed and I laughed a little, which broke the ice.

"What is it?"

"Oh," she said. "Blue."

"Wow, you know, that's my favorite, too." I pointed out some blue on the wall paintings. Maya was stroking the stuffed dog's fur, not really looking at me.

"You like the dog, huh? I love dogs. Do you have a favorite baby doll?"

"I don't know," she said. "I don't have one."

I couldn't believe it. How could a four-year-old girl not have a baby doll? It seemed like such a basic thing. But it explained every-thing.

I have no memory of any blanket, stuffed animal, or toy from my childhood. It just added to the feeling that I wasn't loved, that no one cared enough to give me one. But it had been so many years and I had put up a wall blocking off that part of my life. Talking to this little girl started to chip away at that wall. I remember what that feeling was like, how it told me how little I was worth.

"Hi—sorry, I couldn't get out of work." I looked up as Reece walked in the door. He introduced himself to Sheri and then went right for the kids. "Helllllooo," he said to the kids, joyful and easy. "You must be Maya. I'm Reece." He was so natural that I hated him for it. But I was relieved he was there—he was a ray of light.

Immediately he sat next to Makai on the floor. "And you must be Makai." When Reece's and Makai's eyes met, it was like a spark in a darkened room: *love at first sight*. Makai's face just opened. Blank before, he was suddenly so present. It was like a transfor-mation. Just some love and attention—even a stranger's—snapped him out of it. This approach would be a map forward with Makai.

Once Reece had settled in, Sheri got into the details: "So, you would be their third home since September." She launched in bluntly, as though the kids weren't even there. "The first foster mother called in and said, 'I can't take these kids; they're awful. They're out of control. They don't listen. The little boy is a biter and the girl pees on everything.' So we had to move them."

Sheri kept on, and I didn't want to interrupt; her insensitivity was mind-boggling. But it echoed everything I knew about the system. What the kids needed or felt was the last thing on her mind, on anyone's mind.

"Then their second foster mother didn't want them anymore because she wasn't getting paid enough money," she explained, doing a little eye roll. I caught Reece's gaze and we both just silently cringed.

Over the course of the evening, Maya slowly started to open up. I saw her messing with the Dora the Explorer backpack and struggling with the zipper. Then she handed it to me, meeting my eyes. "Can you open it, please?" she asked.

I unzipped it for her and handed it back. "Thank you," she said in a soft voice, almost a whisper. She had decided I was okay, that maybe she could trust me. I was struck by this unfamiliar feeling—a feeling of being needed. I didn't even know how much I craved it, how much I needed it.

As we all started to get comfortable, I breathed a little easier. Then Makai pulled himself up on the couch, crawled over to Maya, and bit her on her upper back. She started wailing and crying; Reece immediately swooped in and picked up Makai. I soothed Maya to get her to calm down and grabbed a cold rag from the kitchen. Sheri went quiet and didn't get up, waiting to see how we would respond.

Reece spoke gently but firmly to Makai, like he'd been a parent for years. "Biting is bad," he said calmly. "We don't bite. Look, biting hurts your sister. Do you see that?" We showed Makai the mark on Maya's back, but he didn't react. Maya gradually calmed down. Unfortunately, I got the feeling that she was used to it.

Ninety minutes flew by. When Sheri said they had to go, I didn't want them to leave. Maya had finally been opening up: playing with the toys, talking to me, asking politely for more food. I looked over, and Makai was letting Reece feed him the little puffs. Everything just felt right.

But then the visit was over.

Sheri scooped them up, and as quickly as they came, they were gone.

•

After they left, there was this quiet, like a void in the house. Our home suddenly felt empty. Reece and I scanned what I would normally call a disaster: toys scattered everywhere, puffs crushed into the carpet, pillows and couch coverings thrown randomly around. It was like a storm had passed through the living room.

"How are you going to feel about this?" Reece asked, gesturing to the wreckage before us. He knew how I liked everything in its place. But the mess felt the opposite to me; I found it beautiful.

"That just doesn't matter," I said. I loved how it felt as if the kids were still there. Their presence remained in that room.

That night, Reece and I barely slept. We lay in bed and talked: *Did they like us? What do you think they're doing now? Are we ready for this? For our lives to change this much?*

We knew that if the kids moved in with us, our life together would be upended. I spent a lot of time at work, and Reece had recently finished some grueling years working full-time while also getting his master's degree. We often spent our weekends at cocktail parties, hobnobbing with senators, doctors, and lawyers; we hosted beautiful dinner parties at our home. Our circle of friends didn't include any parents, and we knew very few neighbors who had kids. People with children seemed to occupy a different universe from our own.

We had lost our illusions about the new world we were entering. We wanted it *so* badly. There in the dark, we were in our own quiet reveries.

"Maya told me she didn't like school," I said. "God, I don't want her to hate school." I knew how much that mattered, how education laid the groundwork for everything else. How school had been the place keeping me together.

"She's four, Rob. She hasn't had a chance to like it. Let's see how she does in the right environment."

Around two in the morning, Reece fell asleep. I got up and peeked into the toddler's room, imagining a little girl in there. And then I went into the nursery and looked into the crib, which also felt suddenly empty. I couldn't stop thinking about Maya and Makai—

what kind of house they were living in, who was taking care of them, who tucked Maya in at night, who picked up Makai when he cried.

My life was curling back in on itself. Years ago, I was an unwanted child who never had a stable home. It would take the kindness of a stranger to make me feel loved. Now things were coming full circle.

•

The next morning, Friday, Reece and I got up around six and had coffee. We talked some more, about how we knew the situation would be temporary, how they'd be reunited with their mom, which was probably best for them. But until then, Reece kept saying that at least they'd have some stability.

I felt myself opening, but to someone like me, that was a scary thing. I was forty-two years old but still fragile, still a kid afraid to lose someone.

It had taken months to even get that first phone call, so we were sure that moving the kids in would take some time.

I showered and got dressed for work. It was going to be a busy weekend—that Tuesday was Barack Obama's first inauguration and an estimated one million people were about to flood into DC. The city was essentially going to shut down for the week. We were invited to some inauguration events and parties, but our plans were about to change.

Five minutes after I got to my office, the phone rang.

"How did you guys sleep?" Sheri asked.

I laughed. "Not at all."

"Sooo, what do you think?"

"What do I *think*? They were amazing. Great kids."

"And? Have you decided?"

"Decided what?"

"If you want to foster them?" she asked.

"Oh, knowing us, I'm sure we're going to spend many more hours talking about it. But we just loved them. Wonderful kids."

"That's great," she said, taking a hesitant breath. "But we need you to make a decision today."

"Excuse me?" I said. *Today?*

"We have to get these kids placed in the new home. You know the city's shutting down all next week."

"Yeah, but—"

"We just feel they're a really good fit for y'all," she said. "But you have to decide today."

I told her I'd have to talk to Reece and call her back. We were being asked to completely transform our life in twenty-four hours. The thought alone made me dizzy.

But once Reece and I spoke, our answer was so easy. It was really no decision at all. We were ready.

· 6 ·

WHERE TO GO

1979

After Mom dies, there's a giant hole in our house and our lives. I like to go into her closet and bury my face in her pink satin pajamas, which still carry her smell. If I close my eyes, I can pretend she's there next to me. She wasn't the ideal mother, or even a good mother, but that doesn't matter once she is gone. She was what I had. Now I only have Frank.

It doesn't take long for Frank to pack up all her things and get rid of them. He says nothing to Beth or me, just loads up the car with boxes of Mom's things and comes back with nothing. I don't even know where he takes them; I picture a strange woman out there, walking down the street wearing Mom's clothes.

Life with Frank is long periods of neglect broken by moments of crippling fear. I'm twelve now, and I feel older, more mature, and less tied to the house. When my mom was sick, one of her neighbor friends, Sue, started to look after me from time to time. Sue was a devoted Mormon in her twenties who had a little baby, Nancy. My mother would coddle and coo over Nancy so much, making me jealous. That's all I ever wanted from my mother, and this woman's baby got it by doing nothing.

To escape Frank, I sometimes run down the street to Sue's house, which is an oasis: calm, warm, and inviting. She feeds me when I am hungry and treats me kindly, asking how I am, talking to me about making good choices and setting goals, listening to me when I talk about school or Frank. I don't spend too much time wondering where her kindness comes from: I am just grateful.

One time I get caught sneaking over to Sue's house, and Frank just loses it.

"It's not right, Terry!" he bellows. "How do you think that looks—a boy going over to a strange woman's house like that?" I think about the millions of things that go on in my house that aren't right. But I say nothing. I don't think Sue is strange; she is the least strange person I know. I've begun to understand that not everyone lives like we do.

Frank puts me on restriction again and forbids me from ever going back there. But I feel less locked in to his commands, more in charge of my freedom. Why does he care, anyway? When Frank is home, he's either ignoring or berating us. He is always in his bedroom, even for dinner, his overflowing ashtray propped on his stomach. I don't say hello when I come into the house and I don't say goodbye when I leave. We are just like passing ghosts at this point. When he leaves for work in the morning, I jump the fence to go to Sue's, where at least I can get breakfast.

A short time later, we pick up and move out of the house. It's the final step, and my mother's memory is wiped from the face of the earth.

•

A few months after Mom dies, Frank brings a woman home. Her name is Valerie and he introduces her to Beth and me as our new mom, as if he just bought a washer or dryer. Valerie is frail and short, under five feet. She has thin hair pulled back in a pony-tail and streaked with gray and carries that same smell that hangs on Frank like cologne—cigarettes and beer. When Valerie comes downstairs in the morning, she can't even address us until she gets to the refrigerator and cracks open a beer. We ask her for breakfast and she just ignores us until at least half a can is drained.

Frank and Valerie's new house is in the same town, but on the outskirts, where there are no neighbors. Valerie brings her three teenage sons to live with us, and they take over the house like wolves—smoking pot and blasting heavy metal and never going to school. The entire feel of the house shifts from mere neglect to something more sinister and dangerous. Those boys seem to bring out the worst in Frank, who becomes more abusive. One day I can't go to school because he is scared about what the teachers—or I—will say about my fresh bruises. But I never say a word. I assume the beatings are all my fault anyway. And I don't want them to get worse.

My sister Beth is the glue keeping me together. Since Fran left—Fran, whom I miss terribly—she's been the one constant in my whole life. I feel like nothing too horrible can happen as long as Beth is there. Since she's been through what I have, she reminds me that I'm not crazy, that this is actually our life. But around the time she turns fifteen, she goes to live with friends and doesn't come back. It feels like another death, and it just shatters me to pieces. I have never felt more alone, and I have no idea how to put myself back together.

I guess I start to carry the fear on my face, because some adults notice. My math teacher and choir teacher can tell things are not right at my home. I don't even have to ask, but they find ways to let me stay with them after school, doing homework in their classrooms. Frank's abuse is never something we talk about, nor do they try to stop it. They're just keeping me as long as they can until I have to return home.

•

I know I'm a feminine boy. In school they call me a sissy, and I try everything within my power to toughen up. To avoid drawing attention, I struggle to learn what I can about sports. On top of everything, I can tell that I'm attracted to other boys. And even though I don't label myself, I know I'm supposed to feel ashamed about it.

In middle school, I hear about a teenager nearby who is caught "touching" another boy. All the neighbor kids talk about it. The parents talk about it. Everyone says to stay away, but I do the opposite. Drawn to him, I become his friend. I find my way over to his house—and keep going back. Another time, a friend's older brother tells me he's an artist and asks if he can show me how to draw the male form, which leads to other things.

One day I walk into the living room as Frank slams down the telephone. He senses my presence and looks up. Then he stares right at me, which is rare, like he's weighing something in his mind.

"Terry," he says. "Guess what?"

I don't know what to say, so I don't respond.

"You know, I've been trying like hell to get in touch with your dad."

"Uh-huh," I say.

"Well," he says, lighting a cigarette and using it to point at the phone. "Just found out he's dead. He died pretty soon after your mom." He gives a light laugh as he says it. At the coincidence, I suppose. I feel nothing and I say nothing.

"So your mom's dead and your dad's dead," he says. He makes it sound like my fault. "Well, shit, Terry, I sure as hell ain't gonna be stuck with you."

My mom's sisters don't talk to Frank anymore, and Uncle Bruce and Aunt Tara don't offer to take me. And he doesn't ask them to. "You can go live anywhere you want," he says, "but I don't want you here anymore."

He tells me not to come home tomorrow. I'm twelve years old.

•

After school the next day, I take a different bus than usual—one to my old neighborhood—and walk over to Sue's house. I ring the doorbell, and when she opens the door and I see her face, I immediately start crying. Throughout the school day, I had been holding it together, but at that moment it all floods out. I can't make the tears stop.

"Terry? Terry, what's wrong?" Sue asks.

I have trouble catching my breath. It takes me a while to get the words out.

"Terry, you can tell me, honey," Sue says.

"I don't know what to do," I tell her. "I have nowhere to go."

"What?" Sue says. "What is it?"

I explain that my dad's dead and that Frank told me not to come back, that I can't live there anymore. She brings me into the house, and I am just standing there crying. *I don't have a family*, I think. *I don't have a home.* She calls her husband, Eddie, who comes home from work.

When Eddie gets there, I sit in the living room listening to the two of them in the kitchen. "We can't just throw him out," she says. "The church tells us so. It says we are hypocrites if we turn away the needy. We have to do something. We have to take care of him."

Eddie doesn't seem excited by the idea, but he doesn't argue. He picks up the rotary phone and calls Frank. I can only hear Eddie's side. "We wanna keep Terry. . . Okay . . . I'll be there . . . Okay." Then he hangs up and turns to Sue. "Frank said he couldn't care less. As far as he's concerned, we can drop Terry off at an orphanage. If we want, we can get his stuff tomorrow."

A silence fills the room. Sue can see how nervous I am and does her best to make me feel welcome. "Okay, well there's time before dinner. You need a real scrubbing. Why don't you go into our bathroom and take a shower?"

I walk along the upstairs hallway, holding a fresh towel in my hands. When I close the door, I am in this strange bathroom. I stare at the green tile for a moment. Then I open the shower curtain and figure out how to turn on the faucet. Once I step in and the water hits, I'm struck by the blue bar of soap on the ledge. The one that Sue and Eddie use on their bodies. It feels like I've crossed a boundary.

Something about that soap makes me stop. I stare at it and something hits me, or more like clicks into place. I realize how different my life is from my friends'—who are at home with their families, using their own bathrooms and eating at their own dinner tables. Not using a stranger's soap. Sue had been nice to me and given me food, but this feels different. It's personal. Even though my mother and father and Frank had all been abusive, they were still my family. These people outside the bathroom door? I don't really know them. I don't know their middle names, their birthdays, their favorite colors. I am a stranger to them.

The first night at Sue and Eddie's, I cry myself to sleep in the basement bedroom. I am grateful for their kindness, but I am in a strange house, and they are strangers. Or maybe I feel like the stranger.

The next day, Saturday, we go to Frank's house and the few things I have are in the front hallway, stuffed in a black trash bag. I toss it in the trunk and we go back to Sue and Eddie's.

Back at the house, Sue is going through the bag, taking out my few ratty T-shirts and pairs of underwear. "There's nothing in here," she says, more to Eddie than to me. She seems baffled. "This is everything? He doesn't even have decent clothes to wear to church tomorrow." She turns to me. "Terry, are there more clothes back at your house?"

I shake my head.

"This is it?"

"Yes," I say, my voice—cracked and quiet—not quite pushing through. I'm embarrassed. Frank and my mother never once took me shopping. My lack of formal clothes feels like my fault. But I'm older, starting to realize how abnormal my life has been up to now.

"It's okay, honey," Sue says. "We'll fix this. You're tall enough to wear Eddie's clothes tomorrow and we'll take you to get some clothes this week."

On Monday, Sue takes me to school to change my contact information and records. The woman in the administration office tells me they have no record that I've gotten my shots.

"How can that be?" Sue asks. "He's *been* going to school here."

They have no idea. But I'm not allowed back in until I get them done.

"What?" Sue asks. "I don't understand. He's *been* going here."

"Sorry," the woman says. "That's policy. He can't attend without immunizations. No one can."

Sue asks me if I remember getting shots, if maybe the school had lost the paperwork. I tell her no, that I have no memory of shots. Actually, I don't remember my mother ever taking me to the doctor at all, but I don't say this.

One of the problems, I start to realize, is that I am not one of *those* kids. There are kids who skip school, cause trouble, and get detention. There are kids who are removed and put in juvie, kids who have social workers checking in on them. Kids who start fights or fires or trouble wherever they go.

But this is not me. I go to school just about every day, get good grades, don't smoke or disrespect my teacher or get violent. I never say a word about what is going on at home. And because I don't bring attention to myself, no one has to look at me. No one knows how much help I need. No one *wants* to know.

I often fantasize about causing a scene, cursing out a teacher, cutting for a week, hitting another student, throwing a chair through a window—glass shattering everywhere, teachers pulling me away. Anything to get someone to notice me. Anything to become a problem so I can then be solved.

Sue's house is back in the same neighborhood where I used to live with my mother and Frank and Beth. All those neighbors know me, but no one says a word. One day I'm just living at another person's house, part of a new family. Their silence makes me feel small.

Small enough to slip through the cracks.

And I keep falling.

· 7 ·

A MOTHER

After spending twelve years at empty and dirty houses, Sue and Eddie's house might as well be an estate. It feels like a real home and is warmly decorated with nice furniture, like a cool coffee table that Eddie made, wrapped in ship's twine. There are three bathrooms, lots of space, and I have a basement bedroom, with bunk beds, that is all my own. Even though it's cold and dark down there, with no windows, I don't care. At least I feel safe. Most nights I lie on the bottom bunk and stare at the brown carpet until my eyes get bleary and I fall asleep.

Good to her word, Sue takes me clothes shopping at Leggett's Department Store, the first such trip in my life. Just getting some shirts and pants—not my cousins', not hand-me-downs, not things that were left behind, but new clothes that are *mine*—makes me feel like I'm worth something. She is generous and kind, buying me my first toy, a race car track with electric controllers you squeeze like a gun.

Even though Sue will have two more children after I move in, she includes me in the family and never forgets my birthday. For one of them, she buys me a yellow ten-speed bike. The bike gives me a new sense of freedom, a feeling like I can go anywhere. I'd always been left on my own, from a young age, but had never really been free.

In the living room, on the chestnut-brown wall unit, is a turntable and a row of vinyl records. I love to sit on the carpet and flip through those covers—they seem like tickets to other worlds: beautiful, romantic worlds full of hope and love, strange men in bizarre outfits and unreal poses. Sue is always playing Elton John, his voice and piano blaring through the speakers. She and I dance around and sing "Tiny Dancer" into hairbrushes. We spend a night laughing like kids at a sleepover as we sit on the couch and peel peaches. Sue is in her midtwenties, but she seems so much older to me. She is like what I imagine a real mother to be, the first one I have ever had.

Sue is a devoted Mormon, which seems to guide a lot of her behavior. Unlike my parents' random, intense periods of church, which felt forced and phony, Sue's religion seems to actually flow through her. The Mormon church is very structured, and the Sunday service is long, practically an all-day affair with men and women sitting on opposite sides of the aisle.

I don't buy into any of the teachings, but I like that it's a giant family who takes care of each other. The sense of community makes me feel like I'm a part of something. Life at Sue and Eddie's house becomes mostly normal, more normal than any life I have known before. We eat dinner as a family at the same time every night, and pray together. Once a week we can't use the phone or see friends so we can dedicate the evening to reading scripture.

Soon, though, Eddie reveals his true self. He holds me down violently and tickles me until I pee my pants, or pins me and starts to spit on me, sucking the saliva up before it drops and then laughing. I feel like I can bear this mild torture. *At least he pays attention to me*, I think. *He cares I exist.* I probably cut him slack because he took me in when he didn't have to. And because my experience had been with the absolute worst collection of father figures imaginable.

I never really feel entirely part of Sue and Eddie's family. I try the best I can to be the perfect kid, never complaining, coming right home from school and making sure everything is in its place. When not at work—babysitting neighbors, doing a paper route, and, later, working nights at a taco place—I'm doing everyone's laundry and making sure the house is clean. My hours are spent vacuuming the carpet; feeding and cleaning up after their cocker spaniel, Taffy; scrubbing the counters; organizing the kitchen; and cleaning the couch. God forbid everything isn't just right when Eddie comes home.

Still, fear hovers over me that they are going to throw me out. Frank had thrown me out, as had my father. There is no doubt in my mind that I'll be thrown out again here. And Eddie somehow holds that threat over me—without ever directly saying a word.

Anywhere we go, Eddie introduces his biological children and then adds, "And this is my foster child," or, "This is the boy we took in." He always points it out. It hurts because it just says aloud what I know they're thinking: *He doesn't belong.* Sue sometimes does it, too—though it feels more accidental—but Eddie does it gleefully; he knows how it gets to me, the reminder that I can go anytime. That I hang by a thread that he's holding.

Eddie's abuse is almost childish, like a school yard bully's—as if his development were arrested and he never aged past thirteen. He hides behind the deck and pings walnuts from the walnut tree at me when I come out, giving me little bruises on my back. Then he cackles as I run back inside.

Sue also has to put up with Eddie's abuse. He is jealous of my relationship with his wife. He goes on these rants about how Sue pays too much attention to me, and he constantly throws in my face what she does for me that he doesn't get. One time, in a rage, he even accuses us of having an affair.

Sue isn't the best housekeeper or cook, and Eddie is always belittling her. He hates that she watches soap operas in the afternoon, and he spews ugly names at her, calling her lazy and fat. When he comes home from work, he goes right to the TV in the bedroom to see what channel it was last on, to check on her. One of my routines becomes switching the channel before Eddie gets home in order to protect her.

One day, Sue sits me down, visibly upset, and says she needs to talk to me. I'm nervous but not surprised. She tells me that she sent away for my birth certificate and just found out that we had been celebrating my birthday on the wrong day. "I'm so sorry, Terry," she says, as she begins to cry. "It's the eighteenth, not the sixteenth."

"Okay," I say.

"I feel so terrible," she says.

"It's okay."

She seems so upset about it that I feel like I should comfort her. It's weird, I think, that she never feels guilty about anything Eddie does, but this small slight seems to really cut her, like it's a cardinal sin.

•

Around the time I turn sixteen, a big change comes over Sue. I'd been there about four years and had a front-row seat to witness things deteriorate in that house. She and Eddie leave the church, their marriage begins to crumble, and she gets a job outside the home for the first time. Eddie is always traveling—I find out later he has a second family—and Sue is out a lot more. I am always watching their three children, Nancy, Steven, and Blake. I'm in charge so much that I become their de facto parent. One Saturday when I'm in high school, Nancy comes into the living room. Sue and Eddie are there right next to me on the couch, but she walks up to me. "Terry," she asks, "can I go play at Karen's house?"

"Sure thing, honey," I say. "Of course." And then she runs off. It doesn't occur to her to ask her parents, and they don't weigh in.

Through all my high school years, I have no friends or social life outside of watching my three foster siblings. I regularly come home from school, pick up Baby Blake, and take him back to school with me for choir or school musical practice. I started doing musicals the year my mother died and participate in about two a year. They allow me to not be home and, more importantly, to not be myself. Disappearing like that is a huge relief, and I find myself seeking out that feeling, feeding off it. On that stage I can be anyone— Huckleberry Finn, Ebenezer Scrooge. I don't have to be Robert.

●

Two weeks after my eighteenth birthday, I am home after school, watching my siblings and folding laundry in Eddie and Sue's room. I open up the bottom drawer to put away Eddie's jeans and see a *Playboy* magazine. I have never seen one before, so I sit on the floor and page through it. I literally have no idea what it is.

It's like the photographs on the vinyl records but more graphic— naked women wearing nothing but cowboy hats or boots. As I'm drawn into these strange pictures, I hear, "Hey! What the fuck, Terry? What are you doing?!"

"I was—"

"What are you— Snooping around my things?!" Eddie is enraged. "Looking in my drawers?"

"I wasn't—"

Eddie grabs the magazine, shoves it back in his drawer, and then he's on top of me, hitting me with his fists. I get out from under him and run out of the room. He chases me, starts pushing me down the hallway, cursing and screaming.

"I want you the fuck out of my house!" he screams. "You're eighteen; we're done with you. Don't come back here, Terry. We don't fucking want you here."

Sue comes home in the middle of the argument. She seems out of it, surprised that Eddie has come home early from his business trip. She's jittery and nervous and looks like she might have been drinking. "What's going on?" she asks.

"I walked in and caught him going through our drawers," Eddie says. "Looking through my stuff."

"That's not true!" I yelled.

"So I'm a fucking liar?"

"No, I was—"

"I'm done with you! Done! You're not our family. *Get out of my house.*"

"Mom," I start, trying to explain, but Eddie shouts over everyone.

"Sue!" he yells. "Tell him I'm not fucking around. He's out of here."

I turn to Sue, the only lifeline I've ever had. The only person who ever chose to be my parent. "Mom?"

She starts crying as she walks over to me and touches my shoulder. "I'm sorry, Terry. You have to leave." She must have known this was coming, because she doesn't even argue. She just seems resigned. "You just have to go," she says quietly.

"Get your shit and get out of my house!" Eddie yells. "Don't fucking come back and don't come see my kids." He has been yelling the whole time, but in my head it's almost like the volume on him has been shut off. Despite having always felt this was coming, I'm still frozen in shock. I walk mechanically down to my basement bedroom, the same one I cried myself to sleep in six years ago, and gather my things. I shove what I can into my school backpack and head to the door.

On my way out, I see Nancy sitting on the floor in the living room. "Bye, Nancy," I say, kissing her on her forehead. "I'll probably never see you again." Then I leave.

•

The *Playboy* thing is just an excuse. Eddie had been planning on throwing me out anyway. He and Sue had been getting money from the state to take care of me all those years, which stopped as soon as I turned eighteen. Once there were no more checks, Eddie had no reason to keep me. When I go to their house the next day after school, all my stuff is out on the porch in a trash bag. Again, my life in a trash bag. I pick it up—the sum total of my life—and walk away.

Fortunately, I have a car, a '73 blue Mustang with bucket seats from Sue's father. He had wanted to give it to me, but Eddie forced him to make me pay for it. It took me some time, but thankfully I had paid up, or else I'd literally be on the street. I get in my car and drive to the first place I can think of.

My sister Beth lives about fifteen minutes away, with two other girls, and I find her town house. "Well, you can't live here, Terry," she says. "I have roommates. They're not going to be cool with you just *living* here."

She speaks so matter-of-factly, so coldly, like she doesn't have space to care about me; she had pulled herself out and I don't matter anymore. "I just rent a room," she says. "I can't have you screw this up." But she's family and her rejection stings, worse than being kicked out of my home.

That first night, I fall asleep crying on the cold leather back seat of my car. The next night I knock on the window of a friend's house, and she lets me sleep on the floor of her room. For almost a week, I couch surf, wearing out my welcome everywhere. A family I had once babysat for lets me sleep on their couch for a week or so, but eventually they apologize, saying I can't stay there any longer because they don't like how it looks.

I get in the habit of sitting at the back tables of the public library until closing. At night, I sleep in my car most of the time, but I feel exposed and unsafe. For a while, I sleep inside the public bathrooms next to the taco place where I work. It's filthy, with these piercing bright lights, and the lock doesn't work, so I sleep curled up on the hard tile between the toilet and the door, my body pressing against it. Sometimes I'm woken up by someone kicking the door or pushing it open. Hidden away from the street, the place is clearly a cruising place, and sometimes men try to force their way in.

In the mornings, I wake up early to the sound of buses and trucks and try to sneak into the school gym to take a shower before class. But the hunger is the worst. That hollow pit in my stomach from a couple of days with nothing to eat hurts more than any abuse. The ache never goes away.

In the senior lounge during lunch, I wait to be the last person to leave because I know there will be food left out on trays or thrown away. I pick through the trash and grab food from abandoned plastic trays—sometimes jamming it all in my mouth quickly or shoving it in my backpack next to my books. Somebody shouts "What happened to my Tater Tots?" as I'm covering my mouth or turning away, hiding what I'm chewing.

I'm living a secret out in the open, but no one can rescue me. No one can help. At school, my choir teachers and a few other teachers know I have no home and sometimes let me stay late. Two of them raise money for me to go on the senior trip, a kindness that touches me, a generosity I'll hold on to during the tougher times—and one I commit to passing forward someday.

During the last few weeks of school, my friend Kimberly convinces her parents to let me sleep on their basement couch. They agree, but they make it clear I have to leave after graduation. If not for their kindness, I would've dropped out.

I have to finish high school—what else am I going to do? Where else am I going to go? It's simply easier to keep going—to have normalcy and a roof over my head and a lunch rather than spend the weekdays on the street. The weekends are the toughest because there's nowhere for me to go. I finish high school mostly out of momentum, and out of a clear sense of fear. I have no idea what will come next.

· 8 ·

THE SADDEST GIRL IN THE WORLD

January 2009

A few hours after hanging up with the social worker, I was driving around a run-down neighborhood in Northwest DC looking for an address. I had grown up in similar areas: broken-down row homes, crowds of people on front porches, the smell of marijuana wafting in the air, more than one guy on the corner drinking alcohol from a brown bag before lunchtime.

I pulled up to an attached two-story house of faded red brick. Walking up to the cluttered front porch, I noticed broken toys and a metal gate. As I got to the door, all the muscles in my body went to jelly. I pressed the doorbell a few times but heard nothing. So I knocked on the aluminum screen door, the sound rattling in the fresh air. I heard the yells of a couple fighting next door and a siren passing in the distance.

An older, heavyset woman wearing a housecoat, like a nightgown with buttons up the front, opened the door. This was Kim Calfee. She reminded me of the kind of stern grandma who would thwack kids on the legs with a switch if they got out of line. (Later, I found out this was exactly what she did.) I got a flash of Shelly, the woman I lived with as a kid who covered me in bruises, the one who made me walk home in girls' underwear.

Grandma Calfee sized me up. "You must be one of those white guys they said were coming to take my babies," she said, direct but friendly. "Come on in."

It was a dark house, cluttered but neat, with lots of knickknacks from dollar stores. There was a layer of dust on everything—the kind of place you can't ever get clean.

A bunch of kids were in the house—a few running around, a couple more sitting on the floor or on blue daybeds up against the walls.

"Oh my gosh. All these kids!" I said.

"Yep. I'm the regular neighborhood nanny. People are always dropping their kids here."

A pronounced smell of cooking grease and urine hung in the front room. I found out later there was no bathroom on the first level, so the kids usually peed in a pot on the back porch.

Makai sat in a mesh playpen, staring at nothing. As I started to make my way to him, I saw at my feet a baby in a car seat, maybe two months old, so I bent down and cooed at him. "Oh my God, he is the cutest little baby."

"Oh, won't be long until that one is in the system, too," Kim said. "His momma lives around the corner; she's fourteen. Always dropping those two off." She gestured to another little boy, maybe two, with cornrows, sitting on the floor in a diaper. "That's his brother." He was just staring off out the window.

Maya came walking around the corner, still not smiling, never smiling. She looked up and recognized me. "Hi, Maya," I said. She began to approach.

"Maya, say hi to Mr. Rob."

"Hi," she muttered.

"Now, get over here and give Grandma a hug goodbye," Kim said. Maya walked into a side hug and disappeared into Kim's body. "Maya, I'll see you. I love you." I leaned over the playpen and picked up Makai. I didn't know at the time that it was rare for children to allow new people to pick them up, but both Maya and Makai were immediately ready to come with me.

"Now, remember," Kim said to me, "you can always bring them to me. I'll watch them. I know how it is." She wrote down her phone number for me. "I've been doing this for thirty years. Once children come into my home, they're my babies."

"Do you have all their stuff together?" I asked.

"Yep," she said, "right there." She pointed to the door and there were two white trash bags with red drawstrings. She yelled for an older boy to take their stuff out to my car. We walked out of that house, Makai on my hip, Maya holding my hand.

Kim wasn't a bad person, and in many ways, the system enabled people like her, those who took in far more children than they could handle. She loved those children, but I know all too well that you love people how you have been taught to love.

•

When I brought the kids home and put Makai down, he immediately went to Reece. First he tried to walk, lifting his legs with his hands. I watched him closely and noticed how his legs were buckled in. Then he gave up and just crawled over to him. Reece picked him up. "C'mere, Makai! Hey, buddy!" Again, Makai's eyes just lit up.

We went upstairs to show the kids their bedrooms, which they hadn't seen on their first visit. Maya's walls were a beautiful shade of yellow and decked out in Disney characters, overflowing with toys and stuffed animals on just about every surface. She was a bit shell-shocked. "This is my room?" she asked.

"Yeah, it's yours," I said, smiling, my voice rising in pitch. "It's your bedroom."

Reece took Makai to show him his room while I went down to get the trash bags out of the car.

When I came back in, I turned to Maya. "Are you hungry, sweetheart? Would you like something to eat?"

"I don't know," she said, but I could tell she did.

"Come here," I said, waving her over playfully.

We opened up the refrigerator, and her eyes bulged out at all the food. "All this is ours?" she asked.

"Everything," I said. "Anything you want you can have."

"I can? Anything?" she asked, scrunching up her nose.

"Anything."

I made Maya a peanut butter and jelly sandwich, and Reece began pulling things out of their trash bags. He shot me one of his you've-got-to-be-kidding-me looks.

"What is it?" I asked from the kitchen.

"There's no toothbrush," he said. "Only one pair of pajamas, no doll, no blanket for Makai." He pulled out some used clothes, most with holes, a pair of once-white footed pajamas, all pilled. The feet of them were so run-down they were translucent.

"You know what?" he said, shoving everything back in the bag. "Forget it. Rob, get the car. We're going shopping."

•

Under the blinding lights of Target, we filled two shopping carts in a cathartic burst: shirts, pants, pajamas, shoes, dresses, toys, and bath toys. If the kids looked at it and we saw something in their eyes, we just threw it in the cart. It was indulgent, but we didn't mean for it to be that way. It was simple: they needed, and we wanted them to have. I thought of that first trip with Sue to get church clothes, how it was so necessary. How something so simple made me feel like I mattered.

That trip to Target was the first time we realized Makai had other difficulties besides walking. After about an hour in the store, he got antsy and started screaming. Bothered by the store's bright lights, he buried his face in Reece's shoulder, even tried to bite him. That experience was the beginning of one long process of learning what Makai needed, how he communicated, and what we could do to help.

At home, we filled the tub and started a bubble bath for Maya. Watching her add the bubbles and dump out her new bath toys, I could see in her eyes that her walls of self-protection were starting to be chipped away. But she still hadn't smiled.

Out in the hallway, I whispered to Reece. "This is the happiest day of my life," I said, my voice breaking. "Next to meeting you, nothing could be better than this. But we're going to have the saddest little girl in the world."

"Well," Reece said, "she has every reason to be sad."

"I know," I said. "I know."

When the bathroom door opened, Maya had her new little pink robe on. In her bedroom, Reece had laid out three new nightgowns on her bed. She picked up the one with three Disney princesses on it and tore the tag off with a satisfied snap. Then she smiled.

From the moment I had met Maya, there was a sadness in her face that seemed permanent. When that smile appeared, it changed her whole face—her eyes, her cheeks. There was a light coming off of her and it transformed that whole room.

"Honey, why are you smiling?" I asked, just so happy to see that she could.

"I never had a new nightgown before."

•

Reece and I took the next week and a half off from our jobs to bond with Maya and Makai. We stopped doing dinner in front of the television and set up family dinner in the dining room every night. We wanted to set a stable routine for the children. We tried to do the same with breakfast, but the madness of the morning made that difficult. Nevertheless, we both consciously tried to shift the feel of the house. We were parents now and decided to do everything we could to communicate that to the children.

When Maya came home from school, I was so excited when she pulled out an assignment. *I'm a dad!* I thought, as we sat down at the table together. *My daughter has homework!*

She handed me the papers and, at the top, written in a kid's big block handwriting, was *AMAYA*.

"They gave her the wrong school papers," I said to Reece. "These say *Amaya*." I leaned down to meet Maya's eyes. "Honey, did you get the wrong school papers?"

"No," she said quietly.

"What do you mean?"

"That's my name," she said.

"Wait. What?" I thought I misheard her.

"That's my name," she said a bit louder.

The declaration was like a whack in the face. "What? Your name is *A*-maya?"

"Yes."

Reece and I met eyes across the kitchen. I put my hand on hers. "Honey, why didn't you tell us?"

She shrugged. "Everyone called me Maya. I thought I was supposed to be Maya."

Hearing her say that broke my heart—four years old and everyone in her life had been calling her by the wrong name. I knew how important a name was, especially for someone without a stable life or home. Reece came around to sit with us, and I took her hands. "I am so, so sorry," I said, meeting her eyes and making sure she knew I meant it. "Listen to me, sweetheart: your name is Amaya, and we will never, ever allow anyone to call you anything different."

The next time the social worker came to the house, I blasted right into her. "Don't you realize that's her name?! How could you get her name wrong?"

"I'm her third social worker," she said, almost waving me off. "I didn't know. It's what it said on the papers." The error wasn't a single person's mistake—it was the result of how the system operated. Amaya wasn't a child to them—just a file. That mistake felt so neglectful and so avoidable. What do you have that's your own if not your name?

•

Two weeks after the children moved in, I found food hidden in Amaya's room. The first time, it was an open bag of Fritos and a container of the puffs that we fed Makai. I didn't think much of it, assuming she just had a snack up there. But then it happened again. And again. Next, I found a couple of pieces of bread under her bed.

I went to Reece. "Amaya's hoarding food," I said.

"What do you mean?"

"She's hoarding food. I found food underneath the bed."

"Wait—what? Why would she do that?" Reece asked. "That doesn't make sense."

But it made perfect sense to me. "Reece, you don't know what it's like," I said. "To be hungry like that. To be so used to being hungry that it's all you know." I had had plenty of times like that— never knowing where my next meal was coming from.

"But she knows we have all this food," Reece said, gesturing to the kitchen.

"That doesn't matter," I said. "She knows what she knows. That doesn't just change. It takes time."

The memory of hunger, that empty hole in your stomach, never goes away. It *never* leaves you. I *still* have it, though I haven't been hungry like that for over thirty years. Reece laughs at me that I'm always going to the grocery store or cooking way too much, but at this point, it's just a comforting reflex.

So we just casually emphasized to Amaya that food was something that she would never have to worry about. After a long time, she would accept it as the truth, trust it as her reality. We made a point of letting her know she could open the refrigerator or cabinet and take whatever she wanted, that there'd always be more tomorrow. Even when Amaya put more food on her plate than I knew she was going to eat, I never said a word. It mattered more to me that she didn't even have to think about it. That fear of being hungry followed me everywhere.

· 9 ·

REUNION

July 1985

I was jolted awake by a crash, the sound of a metal trash can being thrown across a hard floor. Then the lights flickered on and the booming voice of the company commander—brusque and charged and filling the room—echoed off the walls. "Get the fuck up! You're fucking ours now! Get your asses out of the bunk!"

It felt like I had just closed my eyes, like I'd just collapsed in an exhausted heap on my thin cot. Through bleary eyes, the barracks came into focus. I glanced around the room, at the same guys I rode the bus there with, young kids as confused as I was. Finally, my brain kicked into gear, and I jumped out of bed and onto the floor.

The commander stepped forward to me. "Seaman Recruit Chasteen! Get your dirty bare feet off my floor!" His voice was like a bucket of cold water. "Put on your issued slippers! Now!"

I quickly obliged and stood back at attention, spine straight and shoulders squared.

Three weeks earlier, I had been sitting in math class and going to choir practice, sleeping on couches and rolling burritos. Now this: boot camp. As I stood there, my mind reasserted itself and pieced everything together in thin strips—giving my car to Fran after graduation, hitchhiking to the processing station in Fort Meade, the day of physicals and paperwork before getting sworn in and being given a motel key and a duffel bag of blue shirts, jeans, and black boots. Throwing away all my tattered clothes in a garbage can. Closing the door of my motel room and the weight—the gigantic weight—that lifted, crying at the relief of *having* a door to close, how nothing and no one could touch me now. The hot shower in which I washed myself raw. How, long after I'd removed all the dirt from my skin, I was still scrubbing, trying to clean myself from the inside. I was cleaning my soul, erasing the nine months with no home, the years of abuse, of never feeling safe, of never having a place of my own. When I got out of the shower, my skin was red and my fingers were wrinkled.

The next morning, I took a flight to Chicago and a bus an hour north to boot camp at Naval Station Great Lakes. There they took our blood and information and lined us up single file and shaved our heads on old leather barber chairs, leaving masses of hair on the floor like discarded rodents.

I was an eighteen-year-old in poor physical shape; this was the absolute last place I belonged. My enlistment was about survival, about clinging to the only life raft I had.

I didn't join the military out of any sense of duty or patriotism. Sadly, like a lot of people, I found the military to be my only respite from an unstable existence. I was there for the safety, the food, and the bed. To escape the streets. For the chance of turning the experience into a line on my résumé and a job, then a normal existence, and then maybe a life. I felt much older than the other recruits, like I had lived ten lifetimes.

"Drop and give me twenty!" My company commander was up in my face, spittle flying.

"Yes, sir!" I did as he said, hands on the cold, gray floor. Some of the kids around me broke into tears. Just the yelling was too much for them. *This is nothing*, I thought. *I can do this.*

I had been saying "Yes, sir" to screaming men since I was old enough to speak. I'd been verbally abused and intimidated since I could walk. This was what I knew.

Next, the chow hall, but by the time we picked up our forks we were being forced out. "Move! Move! You're done!"

I could see the faces and hear the muttered complaints on the other recruits' faces, but I was immune. Men had been touching me and putting cigarettes out on me and whipping me with belts my whole life. I could deal with all of it.

At least I would get something in return for putting up with this abuse.

•

The navy tried to teach me how to take care of myself, which I had already been doing. But it did give me structure and camaraderie and direction. I was a well-behaved kid, polite and hardworking, and eventually voted the honor man in my company.

When my commander found out I was good at typing, I became the division yeoman and didn't have to do the same physical tasks the other recruits did. While they were drilling and doing inspections, I was typing reports, doing dictation, filing for my superiors. I graduated from boot camp with honors, which meant I got to pick my own armed services finishing school. I went into clerical work because I wanted a job, something that would sustain me for life. But my past came back to bite me once again.

After boot camp, we were all hit with another exhaustive round of physical exams and various tests. The navy doctors found blood in my urine and continued to find more with each test. It became harder and harder for me to go to the bathroom. One morning when I woke up, the abdominal pain was unbearable, like I'd been stabbed in the pelvis. My bladder had ruptured, and I was rushed into surgery. The next few days were a blur.

A few days later, lying in a Milwaukee hotel room recovering, I flashed back to all the times my dad hadn't let me go to the bathroom, how he had said only bad kids urinated, how Sue had taken me to a doctor who told me I had nerve damage, how I still held my urine out of habit as a teenager, how Sue used to set a timer and make me pee because I wouldn't do it otherwise. I was completely cut off from my own body, and from one of the most natural feelings in the world. Though he'd been dead for several years, my father was still causing me damage.

When I returned to the base, my petty officer didn't mince words: I was to be medically discharged. It was devastating news. My arguments didn't move him at all—the navy had no use for me. Now my one path to a normal life had been closed off, and there was not a single thing I could do about it.

•

I was nineteen years old, and the navy gave me a manila envelope with a plane ticket back to DC and four weeks' pay. I found a motel in Virginia and paid forty-five dollars a week for four weeks. Every day, I inched closer to being homeless again. I had to do something—immediately. The urgency was a palpable force rising up in me.

So I hitchhiked into town and got a job at a department store. Taking every shift I could and saving every penny, I got enough for the first month's rent at an efficiency apartment. I took a bus out to the local public library, researched how to write a résumé, and typed one up—fudging about college credits. Then I got the local newspaper, flipped to the classifieds, and wrote a bunch of cover letters to any job I thought I could do. First I got a telemarketing job, working nights and weekends, while also waiting tables at a restaurant across the street during the day. After that, I began a job at a local magazine publishing company, eventually working my way to becoming their marketing director.

A few years into my time at the company, a young woman walked in to interview with me for a job. As I looked over her list of references, I stopped short as I spotted a name and a phone number. *Sue.* Everything froze.

"Everything okay?" the interviewee asked.

"What? Yes, yes. Sorry. This Sue Shaw—does she live in Virginia?"

"She used to—but she lives in Maryland now," she said.

"Three kids?"

"Yes, that's her."

After she left, I kept that piece of paper at the corner of my desk. I thought about it the rest of the day into the nighttime and into the next morning. I knew I would end up calling her, but I still didn't know what to say. *What could I say? What would she say?*

The next day on my lunch break, I picked up the phone and called the number quickly before I had a chance to back out.

"Hello?" a voice answered.

"Mom, it's me."

Silence. Then, "Terry?"

"Yeah, it's me."

"Where are you?"

I couldn't even answer her. Just the sound of Sue's voice shot through me. It tapped into this longing that was inside me, dormant but also very much alive.

She said she didn't think she'd hear from me again and that she'd finally left Eddie. There was an element of *you'll be happy to hear it* in the way she said it. And I was. For her.

"Could you come see me and the kids this weekend?" she asked. I could hear something in her voice, something heavy.

"Of course," I said.

•

When I went to visit that Saturday, I was so nervous I thought I was going to throw up on the way. I hadn't seen Sue or the kids in four years—which, at twenty-two, felt like a lifetime. I had passed through a few worlds since the day I left that house.

I pulled up in front of the address she'd given me—a modest town house with big bushes in front. Walking up the steps, I heard two cocker spaniels barking like crazy and saw my brothers and sister scamper to open the door. When they did, everyone—kids and dogs—pounced on me. Mom came around the corner from the kitchen to the hallway and started crying. And we all hugged. I just breathed it all in. Though I had never seen this house in my life, I felt like I was home. For the first time in a long time. If I could have lived inside that exact moment forever, I would have.

Then I turned the corner into the kitchen, and that feeling vanished. I was stunned. *Eddie*. Sitting there, no different than the last time I saw him. Blindsided, not at all expecting to see him, I couldn't think of a word to say. There was an awkward pause, the discomfort hanging thick in that room.

"Terry, give your dad a hug," Sue said.

My feet felt frozen, but I forced myself to walk over and give him a perfunctory hug. Everyone was acting like nothing had happened, like Eddie had never beaten me up, treated me like dirt, and thrown me out on the street. It was almost surreal.

Sue didn't tell me he'd be there, of course, because she was afraid I wouldn't have come. My feelings didn't count—again. I was twenty-two years old, and we were again going to go through this charade of a perfect family. I had belonged to the most dysfunctional families on the face of the earth, yet I was the only one who seemed to realize it.

As my stomach stirred and I built up the rage to say something, I looked down at my siblings and all my anger just melted away. I could see it in their eyes: *they had missed me*. Nancy, almost a teenager now, was holding on to me. "Are you gonna stay, Terry?" she asked. "How long are you gonna be here?"

Steven was pulling my arm to get me to come see his new toy. Their youngest, Blake, had been in a playpen when I left, and now he was this walking, talking child with a personality all his own. They missed their big brother. And I missed them.

After a few more Saturday visits and spending the weekend without Eddie there, I saw that Sue was really struggling. She had been hiding it, but the truth was too heavy and she couldn't pretend any longer. The house was dirty and cluttered, and I'd hear about financial problems she was having, work and home issues that were making her stressed. She was having trouble on her own dealing with my siblings, especially Nancy, who was running that house. A lot of the problem was that Sue had been so beaten down. She was still letting Eddie come over on the weekend to see the kids, and he was constantly demeaning her, stripping away any bits of self-esteem she had managed to rebuild in herself.

During a lull in one of my visits, as we prepared for dinner, Sue stopped chopping vegetables and looked at me. The kids were running around in the backyard, their high voices passing through the thin walls. I had been enjoying the sounds of family around me. My life had been quiet for many years—I lived a lonely life—and the noise was welcome.

"What?" I said. Standing at the refrigerator, I could see that Sue wanted to say something.

"You should just move home, Terry. Just quit your job and move here."

It wasn't like I hadn't thought about it. "I don't know, Mom," I said. "It took a while to find this job and I'm doing well—"

"But I'm sure you could find something better here, Terry."

"Mom, I'm doing okay. I just—"

She took a few steps toward me. "Sorry. I mean *I* want you to move home. I need you to move home." Her voice started to break. "Can you come home?"

That was all she needed to say. The thought that someone needed me—and *wanted* me—was all I ever really wanted. I also had a sense of duty, that feeling that I owed her. How could I say no to this woman who had essentially saved my life? I gave notice at work, rented a U-Haul, packed up my small apartment, and moved in with Sue and the kids. I didn't even have to think twice about it.

· 10 ·

BOYS

March 2009

When Amaya and Makai first came to our home, the judge in their case determined that their primary goal was "reunification" with their mother, something Reece and I completely supported. Their mother, Nora, was doing weekly supervised visitations and had checked herself into parenting classes, drug rehabilitation, and anger management. All signs pointed toward reunification; we focused on just giving the children the best home life possible while we had them.

It was difficult, confusing even, focusing so completely on the present like that. We were building a bond with Amaya and Makai and simultaneously preparing for the day when they would leave. Sometimes I'd lie awake at night and stare at the ceiling, just thinking about how we might never see them again. I couldn't even measure the hole that they would leave in my life.

I tried to put the thought in the back of my mind, but it was difficult. I carried serious abandonment issues, so there was a part of me that was so scared to let my guard down, afraid to openly love these children as much as my heart wanted to. I had covered myself in armor that was hard to take off. What got me through it all was Reece. His heart was wide open and just watching him with Amaya and Makai brought me comfort. He'd help Amaya with her reading and tickle Makai, and their natural connection reassured me we would all be okay.

At first, Amaya and Makai's social workers picked them up to take them to their visitations with their mother and things like doctor's appointments. But soon Reece and I made the decision that, at least for now, we were their parents, so those tasks were our responsibilities. "You tell us where they need to be," I said, "and we'll be there."

For visitations with their mother, we'd pick up Makai from day care and Amaya from preschool. We'd meet the social worker in the parking lot of the community center and wait for an hour or so in the car until the kids came back out.

One time, we were waiting with the kids in the parking lot for the social worker to show up, when a young woman in her early twenties, petite with no makeup, walked up to our car and knocked on our window.

I rolled down the window and said, "Excuse me?"

"I'm their mom," she said, curt and a bit rough, pointing to the kids in the back.

"Oh, hi! I'm Rob, and this is Reece. Nice to meet you." I had never met her face-to-face, so I didn't know who she was.

She nodded. "Those are my babies," she said. "I'd like them now."

"Sorry," I said, awkwardly looking over at Reece. "We're supposed to wait until the social worker gets here." The procedure had been explicitly stated to us, and Reece and I were sticklers for the rules. We never wanted to give the district any reason to deny us anything for the children.

"Excuse me," Nora said. "But these are my children." She tapped on the back window, and Amaya gave her a shy wave.

"I really think we should just wait," I said again, as apologetically as possible.

She walked off, cussing under her breath as she went into the building. I felt for her, but there was nothing I could do. Reece and I often spoke about how we wanted Nora to be part of our lives as well, but those interactions made us feel guilty. Like we were doing something wrong. It wouldn't be the first time we were made to feel this way—and it wasn't just from Nora.

•

Grandma Calfee had a big heart. I could tell when I first picked up Amaya and Makai at her house and practically had to step over all the children. She wanted to love every single kid in the neighborhood, taking on far more than she could handle. Since I'd brought in Amaya and Makai, she and I had been keeping in touch, and she had watched them a few times while Reece and I first figured out day care.

About two months after the kids came to live with us, she called me up.

"Remember that baby boy I was watching when you came over that first time?" she asked. "And the other boy running around with the cornrows—his brother?"

"Of course," I said. I had been thinking about them—something about the baby especially was burned into my memory.

"Well, they're in the system now," she said, "and their mom wants to meet you. She wants to see if you'll take them."

•

"Four kids?" Reece said when I told him about it. I understood his reaction, and to an extent, I agreed with his hesitation. He didn't want to complicate what was already a new and fragile relationship with Amaya and Makai. We were just figuring out how to be parents, and the kids were just getting accustomed to us.

But he hadn't seen those boys. I had.

I know Reece well, so I tried to be as direct as I could. "You just can't say no so quickly," I said. "They need us, Reece. Who else do they have?"

The look on his face said it all: he was the one who had had to convince me to adopt locally in the first place, and now he'd created a monster. Reece took the rational tack. "We already have two kids," he said, "and we don't even know enough about them yet. Rob—"

"I know."

"Life is crazy as it is," he said.

"I know," I said. "I know." What could I say? Reece was right. Reece was always right.

But that didn't mean I was ready to give in. I knew that in a battle between my brain and my heart, my heart was always going to win out. So I let the idea sit. And as I did, I started thinking about those two boys the same way I had thought about Amaya and Makai after our first meeting. Once I laid my eyes on them, I couldn't stop thinking about them.

A week later, Grandma Calfee called again. "What do you think, Rob?" she asked. "I know you just got Amaya and Makai, but these kids . . . these kids need you, honey."

I already knew the boys' story. Grandma Calfee had told me that there was no way their mother was getting the boys back and neither of their fathers seemed interested in getting involved. The older boy, Greyson, had already been in the system once before when he was a baby; he had shaken baby syndrome and bleeding in the brain. But the district had given Greyson back to his mother when he was a year old. Soon after he returned, she broke three of his ribs and put him in the hospital. So he was taken away again. He was now two, and there was almost no chance he was going to be placed back with his mother a third time.

The baby, Tristan, had also recently been taken from their mother. She and Tristan's father were fighting on Georgia Avenue in broad daylight when she took a razor blade and tried to carve the father's initials into the baby to brand him. A police officer saw it happen and took Tristan away on the spot.

Greyson and Tristan were going into the system and they would not likely come out. The tracks of their future were being laid down in front of them, and I started to feel like it was my duty to do something. We had a chance to change their course. To make sure they landed with us—people who could care about them and could take care of them. I knew the other options were harrowing. We had to try.

•

A few weeks later, Grandma Calfee called me at work, saying that the boys' mother, Rose, was at her house. Would I come by and meet her? I asked my boss, and he was sympathetic, telling me to go. I ran out to the parking lot, got in my car, and drove over there. When I got to Grandma Calfee's, Rose was sitting on the front porch, braiding her own hair. I walked up the steps and introduced myself.

"Hi," I said. "I'm Rob Chasteen."

She quietly took my hand, her eyes lighting up a bit. "Hi," she said shyly. Rose had just turned fifteen, but she looked older: she was scantily clad, wearing way more makeup than you often see on a teenager.

Grandma Calfee came out onto the porch and took the lead. She recounted the conversation that she had had with Rose, how the boys' mother was concerned about where the boys would end up. As the three of us got to talking, Rose seemed to warm up to me.

"I know you took those other two kids, and Grandma Calfee says you're good people," Rose said. "And I don't like the woman who's got them now," she said, meaning their new foster mother, who'd had them for a couple of months. "I want you to take my boys. As long as you promise me that you'll get them an education."

I was taken aback by how certain she seemed. She didn't even know me. "Well," I said, not wanting to commit to anything, "I'm more than happy to give all my information to your social worker, to continue this conversation."

It was strange having this intimate and personal conversation with someone I'd just met. With the future of two little boys hanging in the balance.

Rose claimed DC had treated her unfairly. She said that her boys were taken from her because she didn't have the proper baby gates in her house. Though I knew this wasn't true, I didn't challenge her. She was protecting herself, and I didn't judge it. I just tried to listen and stay open. For some reason, she trusted me, and it seemed important to keep that trust in place.

I talked about how if we did take them, we would want Rose to be part of their lives and, eventually, our lives as well. Reece and I both thought that a mother should never be permanently kept from knowing her children. Once Rose got on her feet, we would open our door to her completely.

"I just want my babies to have everything," Rose said.

"Of course, sweetie. We all do," Grandma Calfee said. "I know it."

"I understand," I said. "Believe me—I do."

"But I don't want anyone to adopt them," Rose said. "I want them to stay in foster care."

Grandma Calfee and I exchanged a look.

"I can't guarantee that, Rose," I told her. "I just don't think it's right for a kid just to stay in foster care forever. It's not a permanent solution."

Rose nodded to herself, though she didn't say that she agreed. I didn't want to get into a confrontation about some future that might not happen, so I let the issue drop. "I trust you guys," she said. "Grandma Calfee loves you all, and I saw how happy those other kids are, and I just want that until . . ." Her voice trailed off.

Rose was just so young. All I kept thinking was that this girl was just a troubled child. Her future was not yet written, and though she clearly had been going through some challenges, it was so un-selfish of her at her age—barely going to school herself—insisting that her boys get a good education. She kept reiterating it—she wanted them to be safe and she wanted them to be educated.

Though I was horrified by what Rose had done to the boys, I tried to think of the big picture: she came from an unhealthy environment, having been in and out of foster care herself and having had Greyson when she was a kid, twelve years old and caught up in dreams of playing house. I wasn't excusing her choices—I don't believe in doing that—but those choices originated from a place that can't be ignored.

That night, when Reece got home, I didn't tell him where I had gone that day, but I broached the subject again of taking in Greyson and Tristan. This time, instead of appealing to just his heart, I went for his head, too.

"You know," I said, "Amaya and Makai are going to reunite with their mother. That's in their plan." Nora had been regularly visiting her kids and seemed to be getting her life back on track.

"I know," Reece said. "You don't have to tell me, Rob. Of course I know."

"But I'm just saying we should think ahead. Think about how long it will take to get another kid when they leave. Greyson and Tristan are not going back to their mother, so they're going to end up somewhere. They're on the fast track for adoption."

Reece was quiet as I watched him consider this.

"And Tristan's less than six months old," I added. "A baby! We always wanted to raise a baby."

Reece's face changed right then, making it clear he was coming around. Plus, the momentum was on my side. Reece was smart enough and knew me well enough to see where the train was rolling. I had my mind set on this, and when that happens, I just don't let go. I'm not capable of it. Plus, I knew that once he saw the boys, put his arms around them, they'd be ours. Reece's heart was just way too big to turn them away. That's one of the things I love about him.

A few days later, I confessed to Reece that I had met Rose at Grandma Calfee's house. I went over the conversation, what she had said, how much meeting her had affected me, how I felt for her, how I wanted to adopt her, too. She was almost begging me to take the boys; it was a cry for help for her children. How could we not respond? She was a wayward soul, and if someone didn't do something for her, then she was going to be a statistic. And if someone like us didn't take the boys, they could end up being statistics, too.

Reece's decision was harder to make than mine. Unlike him, I came from a giant family, had then been taken in by a family of Mormons—who traditionally have large families—and had always wanted a big family. The idea of four kids sounded exciting and fun to me. But Reece was home with the kids more, too; he was already dealing with two children, and Makai had special needs, so the days could be overwhelming. I was torn between not wanting to push Reece into it and not being able to push the boys away.

•

For months we never said no, but I couldn't say yes. Reece was just not on board—yet. The whole time, I talked to Grandma Calfee and social workers and kept Reece abreast of what was going on. I bounced back and forth between telling Grandma Calfee we were interested and going to Reece and hearing, "We need to get more information. We need to talk to Amaya and Makai." It felt like it could eternally go on like this, which I just found unacceptable. Even as I tried to take action, I kept getting boxed in, trapped by walls on all sides.

DC, it seemed, was going to be one of those walls. We were hearing that there was a limit for the number of kids under the age of three allowed in a home—that if we brought in Greyson and Tristan, Amaya and Makai would have to be moved, which was obviously a deal breaker. The last thing we were going to do was upend their lives again.

I stalled, dragged my feet, and tried to figure out how I could get Reece across that finish line. Then, one evening, the phone rang. Greyson and Tristan's social worker was on the line, and she told me they were all having an extended family meeting to discuss the boys' future. That night. And I should go.

I picked up Grandma Calfee, and we pulled up to a church in Northwest DC. We found the banquet hall, which was a type of cafeteria, where on metal chairs at various tables sat Rose with her sister and mother, Greyson's dad's parents, a few social workers, the guardian ad litem (an attorney who represents the children's interests), the foster mother, and the minister of the church.

I quietly took a seat with Grandma Calfee at a back table, aware of how much I stuck out, the only white person in the room. Everyone's eyes peeked over to me. The heat of their stares was not an uncommon feeling for me—both during the adoption process and, really, throughout my whole life. I just tried to block it out and remember why I was there. Grandma Calfee must've felt it, too. She gently put her hand over mine and squeezed.

The social worker took control of the meeting and had everyone introduce themselves. She thanked us all for coming, explained that we were going to try to sort out the situation and how "we all want what's best for Greyson and Tristan." Then she wrote the boys' names in black marker on a whiteboard. Underneath that, she wrote *GOALS* and *PLACEMENT*.

The futures of two children were going to be decided in that cold and indifferent room, with industrial fluorescent lights and the dull hum of various appliances. Everyone was hemming and hawing, not volunteering for anything, like a classroom of kids afraid of being called on because they didn't know the answer. And these weren't strangers—these were family members. If no one in this room would do something for these boys, then who in the world was going to?

At first uncomfortable, it quickly became infuriating. Greyson's grandparents said they could take them eventually, but they needed time to first sort things out. Rose's sister said she'd take one but not both, and she preferred Tristan, not Greyson. The foster mother didn't say a word. No one wanted to be there; they were acting like this meeting was a burden—I could tell that attitude would extend to how they would all parent. If one meeting was a hassle, I could only imagine how hard it would be for the kids to get what they needed in daily life.

It was my childhood all over again, and I just couldn't take it. I was fuming. So I stood up and said, "We'll take them."

"Mr. Chasteen," the social worker said, a bit surprised. "Thank you. That's a nice offer. Well, we can look into starting that path . . ."

"No, no," I said dismissively. I couldn't take one more second of the meeting. "We'll take them. We'll figure it out."

•

On the ride home I felt hopeful and exhilarated and relieved. After months of push and pull, I had made an actual decision. Right after I spoke up, Rose immediately supported me. "I want my boys to go with Rob," she told the group, flashing me a weak smile. Just looking in her eyes, I felt like the meeting was taking a toll on her, too.

But now I had to go home and tell Reece. And he was going to kill me.

I love Reece unconditionally, and he's the most impressive person I've ever met, but he's human. Of course he was annoyed, and he had every right to be: I had made a gigantic decision without him.

"But you wouldn't have said yes!" I said in a lame effort at defending myself.

"Yeah, that's the point, Rob," Reece replied. "It has to be both of us making a decision. That's how it's supposed to be."

I didn't have a leg to stand on; of course he was right. But this was not a brain issue—it was a heart issue. I understood what Reece was thinking, but he had to think about what I was feeling.

"I know," I said. "You're right. I'm sorry. It's just that if you were there . . ." I let my words just hang there, not pushing much. He had to come to it on his own. Everything I knew about Reece told me he would.

The emotions of those months had been overwhelming, all culminating in that meeting at the church. That night I cried myself to sleep—because I had hurt the man I loved, because I was so in love with Amaya and Makai and was haunted by the lives they had led, because Greyson and Tristan were now part of my life and I couldn't unknow them.

Another night, I thought, that these boys were living somewhere they shouldn't be living, sleeping somewhere they shouldn't be sleeping. I couldn't stop thinking about what they were going through—the visitations, the foster mother's home, their mother's abuse. I could not—would not—turn them away.

Reece wasn't wrong, though: there was a delicate balance in the house with Amaya and Makai that we had to be sensitive to. And I didn't want to damage what we had built so far, either. A family doesn't just happen when people live under a roof together. It takes time and attention. There are thousands of little things that have to click and coexist before a sense of security and trust and love can evolve.

Makai wasn't really verbal yet, so I sat down with Amaya to talk about Greyson and Tristan. She was a naturally bright girl and though she still had memories of a rough life, she seemed to feel safe and loved. Amaya was always willing to share and was grateful for things big and small, whether it was a cookie after dinner or the Shih Tzu we got her for Easter. I thought of her as my daughter and I just loved her to pieces.

"How would you feel about Greyson and Tristan coming over for a visit?"

"Here?" Her eyes lit up.

"Yeah," I said.

She remembered the boys from Grandma Calfee's house and was super excited. I didn't go further than that—a visit—because we had no idea how it was going to play out. Providing stability for Amaya and Makai was one of the things we had signed up for.

"We'd first like to take the boys for the day," I told the social worker. "Reece wants to make sure that Amaya and Makai do not feel slighted. We want them all to meet and see if everyone is a fit before we continue."

She said she understood. Once again, I was given an address where the children were so I could pick them up. Though I enjoyed spending that car time with the kids, something about this part of the process always left a bad taste in my mouth. I just hated the message it sent. Having the new guardian pick up the kids seemed to represent all the problems with how the district looked after these children. *You get them. They're your problem now.* That message filtered down to how those kids were treated—like an errand on a list or someone else's issue. Like a problem.

I drove out to a house in Maryland and picked up Greyson and Tristan from their foster mother. The kids were both excited—Tristan smiled and patted my chin as I buckled him into the car seat. Greyson, who was two, had a big smile plastered on his face the whole ride back to DC. He said he remembered me from when I picked up Amaya and Makai from Grandma Calfee's house.

In the car, I tried to get Greyson talking, which was easy because he was a gregarious and animated child. Though I couldn't know what was in his heart, he seemed to carry none of the scars from the horrors that had happened to him. He just seemed like a happy boy who loved to talk.

"Do you like animals?" I asked him.

"Yes!"

"Which are your favorites?"

"Zebras. And elephants and cheeters," he said, smiling. "And zebras!" Then he started into a singsong: "Zeee-bra. Zeee-bra-ah . . ."

"Well, you know there's a zoo near our house we can go to sometime. Would you like that?"

"Yes!" he said. "Yes, yes. Now?"

"No, next time. But you know we have a dog you can play with? Two dogs now."

"You do? And dogs!" he said, adding to his list of favorite animals.

"We have Bailey. He's big."

"Bailey, Bailey, Bailey," Greyson said as he looked out the window, getting the feel for the name on his tongue.

"He's a Dalmatian, with brown spots," I said.

"Bailey," Greyson repeated.

"And Amaya just got a new puppy named Kai-lan," I said.

"Yeah! Puppy! Pu-uh-ppy!"

"Do you remember Amaya and Makai?"

"Yes! At Grandma's!"

"They're excited to see you!"

He started throwing himself forward and back in his car seat in excitement, and I laughed. Then Tristan made a gurgly baby laugh.

"Are you hungry?" I asked.

"Yes!" Greyson said. "Hu-uh-ungry," he singsonged. Everything seemed to make him happy. I didn't know yet if this was his personality or if he was just excited about the day's trip.

I reached back to pass Greyson the container of strawberry puffs that we fed Makai. "Tristan! Tristan, here!" he said, and I watched in the rearview mirror as he gave one to his brother before he took one for himself. Even at such a young age, Greyson had a kind soul. I put on the kids music CD we played for Amaya and Makai, and Greyson clapped and repeated words the whole way home.

When we came into the house, Reece was standing in the kitchen. He looked at Tristan, put his arms out, and took him from me. I could see the way Reece looked at Tristan, this adorable baby with eyes that lit up like stars, a boy who just wanted to be loved. This was the way it was supposed to be. Like these boys had come home.

Most babies, when they're given to someone they do not know, cry and resist; they react to a strange face. Tristan wasn't like that. He wanted somebody to hold him. As we got to know him better, we saw that he would go to just about anybody, which was something we had to be careful with. But he was missing something, and he wanted the gap filled.

Amaya and Makai immediately went over to play with Tristan and coo over him. Then they took Greyson to see their toys. I love that about children—there's no get-to-know-you phase. They can simply dive right in. Greyson took Makai under his wing almost immediately. They shared toys and even though Makai would lash out, Greyson kept forgiving him, like he sensed Makai needed him. Greyson talked to Makai even though Makai would not talk back, which most adults didn't even do. The boys seemed to understand each other—they already seemed like brothers.

That afternoon, Amaya suggested that we all bake a cake, and by the time we put it in the oven, the kitchen looked like a bomb had gone off. I was having too much fun to care, and instead of cleaning up—my normal reaction—I suggested we all go for a short walk around the block until it was ready. Hooking the leashes on the dogs, putting Makai and Tristan in the double stroller, we all filed outside.

As we were walking through the neighborhood, laughing and pointing, trying to keep up with Greyson's stories and Amaya's questions, we saw some neighbors we knew walking toward us. They looked slightly perplexed at the additional children. As they came over to say hello, Bailey took charge, taking his eighty-pound body and positioning himself in front of the four kids. Bailey was old and prone to biting, so I had been fearful of how he would be around the kids. Almost immediately, though, Makai or Amaya would just be eating a snack and lean back on the dog like he was an overstuffed pillow. And in that moment on the street, he showed us he was looking out for them.

"Sorry," I apologized, trying to bring Bailey to heel. "He's very protective of the children."

"It's okay," the woman said. "That's good."

Later, we went shopping in DC, then out to a Mexican restaurant for dinner. By the time we settled in at the table, getting three of the kids into high chairs and sorting out who wanted to eat what, fifteen minutes had passed. It was our first experience with four kids in a restaurant. I felt the stares, which were more awkward for me than for Reece. People were trying to figure out what these two white men were doing with four young African American kids. I didn't feel judged so much as just looked at; I felt the intense curiosity carrying across the dining room. Like we were a puzzle to be solved.

•

The next week the boys had their first weekend visit with us. I picked Greyson and Tristan up again in Maryland. Their foster mother was nice enough, a single woman living alone in a cold and cluttered house. In that messy space, she seemed overwhelmed.

Her house had baby gates everywhere and old toys scattered on the floor. I sat at her kitchen table and had a cup of coffee with her, listening to her complain about the system. Anytime I shifted the conversation to Greyson and Tristan, she found a way to spin it into something else.

She packed virtually nothing for the kids—she probably didn't have anything to pack—and I tried to get out of there as soon as possible. There was this negativity hanging on her. It reinforced why we were taking Greyson and Tristan, how much that weekend would matter to them.

That first weekend with all the kids was magical. The six of us went out for pizza, shopped at the mall, played at the park, and pushed Tristan around in a baby carriage. Amaya was so great with Tristan; she had always been drawn to babies, naturally taking care of them and being motherly. Reece was too in love with Tristan to put him down. We made sure Makai didn't feel slighted, like someone was replacing him, so we sat on the floor and played with him, making sure that one of us was right there holding his hand.

On one of my first dates with Reece, we had gone to the zoo, where I bought him a stuffed cheetah. We'd had that cheetah on a shelf for years, but when Greyson came that weekend, we gave it to him. He just about lost his mind, sleeping with it and bringing it everywhere.

That night I sat on the brown leather couch, toys strewn everywhere, with Reece and all four kids, reading *The Giving Tree*, one of my favorite books. Reece was giving Tristan his bottle, and the other three curled around me in their new pajamas. There was no bickering over "mine," no distance or competing for attention. It felt like it was meant to be, like we'd always been together.

That Sunday morning, when it was time for me to take the boys home, I found Amaya crying on the couch. "Hey, sweetie, what's wrong?" For a moment I was worried that we had been giving Greyson and Tristan too much attention. Like we had made her feel less important. "You can tell me what's wrong."

Amaya looked up at me with those big, brown eyes. "I don't want them to leave," she said.

●

"I don't like it, Rob. It's not a good idea," my mom's new husband was telling me on the phone. Sue's husband was just echoing what Reece and I were hearing from all our family members. For some reason, everyone felt very comfortable telling us we were wrong for taking in Greyson and Tristan. "You are not doing the right thing by anyone," he said.

"What does that mean?" I asked.

"It means you're taking on more than you can handle," he said. We heard this from my mother, and from Reece's parents as well. That we weren't going to be able to give the kids what they needed, that we were spreading ourselves too thin, that we just couldn't handle it all.

"Lots of families have four kids," I would say.

"Yeah, but you can't afford them," someone would say.

"But my mom had three kids and then chose to bring me into her home," I'd say. "She and Eddie didn't have a lot of money, either. She wasn't even working when I moved in, and Reece and I have two incomes."

"You don't know what you're getting into," someone else would say. "Those kids—they have issues."

"Yeah, they have baggage," I'd respond, defensive. "So do I. We all do."

That is the point, I was thinking. *That is exactly the point.* These kids had baggage that they had not an ounce of responsibility for. *Isn't this what we're supposed to do for others? We have and we want to share. The kids have so little and want to be loved. What's the problem here?*

The pushback was surprising and hurtful: Who's to say we can't do this? That two kids are okay but four kids is somehow irresponsible? I don't tell anyone how many children they can bear, so why are people telling me I'm doing a disservice to my children? Reece and I were not impulsive people and we were not under any illusions. We had fully considered everything about having four kids, how it would change our lives entirely, and we wanted to do it. The judgment from our families was infuriating.

Dealing with all those responses—standing up to everyone— was a big step for me as well. For the first time in my life, my concern wasn't about making my mother and the rest of the family happy. I had been the constant pleaser, making so many choices with an eye toward what they said or would say. I had broken free of that and was proving it to myself. These children needed me, and I needed them. I didn't care what anyone but Reece thought or said.

I didn't hold it against my mom for worrying. She's a loving person and just wanted what was best for me. Worrying is what parents do. I had stumbled along a rocky road, and for a long time after I had gotten back on my feet, she still worried. She understood what it took to get to where I was in life. And she was always afraid that I would break.

But I let all their words run off me, and with Reece on board, we pushed forward.

Then we ran into another wall.

•

The District of Columbia denied us the boys. The woman in charge of social services at DC Child and Family Services clearly didn't like Reece and me. Even though she knew that Rose had specifically requested that Greyson and Tristan be placed with us, she still said no. It was baffling, another example of the system's inability to look at what truly mattered. No one else was offering to take these kids. We were able to provide for them and we wanted them. We'd been through it all before. The only explanation was that we were white and gay. No other reasons made sense.

It didn't help that I wasn't exactly the most popular person down at DC Child and Family Services. Reece and I rocked the boat too much. Anytime a service didn't happen for Amaya and Makai, or was too slow to happen, I was on their doorstep making noise about the hideous childcare they provided, the medical specialists they refused to approve for Makai, or the regulations that never seemed to serve the kids.

Our social worker would tell us flat out that the head of social services didn't like us. "You're causing way too much trouble," she'd say. "They're always talking about how 'Mr. Chasteen's called again' and how 'he just needs to let things go through' and 'he needs to realize he's not their father.'"

The reason the head of social services gave for denying us the boys was the DC "law" that no foster family could have more than two kids aged two and under. But no one could find this rule in the books. Even the head of the National Center for Children and Families didn't know anything about it. Eventually, we got them to admit that it was more like an unspoken rule. After that, social services stopped returning my calls. So I went straight to the top. We had come too far, and I wasn't going to be denied the boys, or have the boys be denied a home, over some unwritten bureaucratic nonsense.

One afternoon, I drove to DC Child and Family Services and asked to see the director.

"Sorry, you have to make an appointment," one of the men in the lobby told me.

"No!" I lashed out. "I've called and I've called, and no one is returning my call!"

I was the crazy man ranting in the lobby, security guards looking at me sideways.

"Look, there's nothing we can do," one guard said. "We're not going to let you upstairs."

This was Washington, DC. You couldn't just storm into buildings like that; you needed a pass to swipe in order to access your floor.

So I waited . . . and I waited . . . and I waited. I paced in the lobby, past the couch and chairs, shoes squeaking on the bright white floors. There was so much action going on in that lobby that no one even took notice. I got on the phone and fumed to Reece, to the kids' social worker, to anyone who would listen.

Around lunchtime, an older gentleman with glasses and a dark gray suit whom I recognized as the director of DC Child and Family Services stepped off the elevator. I walked right up to him. "Excuse me," I said, "my name is Rob Chasteen and I really need your help."

And before he could respond, I launched into my story. I didn't take a breath and just kept talking and talking, my voice pitched high from the frustration. "It's just not acceptable," I pleaded. "All we want is to bring the boys into our home!" To my surprise, he seemed moved—maybe more by how upset I was than anything else.

"I promise I'm going to look into this," he said. "I'll do what I can to see what's going on here."

A week or so later, everything flipped. DC Child and Family Services not only agreed to place Greyson and Tristan in our care, but they moved our entire case, including Amaya and Makai's case, to a private agency. We had caused so much trouble for them that they wiped their hands clean of us. Reece and I were so relieved to be free. There would be plenty of other battles in the future, but pretty soon, we were going to be able to bring the boys into our home.

That summer, while finishing up the final paperwork for Greyson and Tristan, we invited Reece's family to join us in the Outer Banks of North Carolina for a week. I put in a request to bring the two boys on vacation with us, because to take the children more than fifty miles out of DC we had to get permission from the birth parents. The agency asked their mother, Rose, and to our shock, she said no.

Although we were a week or so away from being their official foster parents, she didn't want us taking them to the beach. She said *she* wanted to be the one to do that. Rose was only fifteen and still held out hope that this was all a temporary setup. She didn't want us to do things with Greyson and Tristan that she wanted to experience with them. Part of me understands that now, but at the time it just felt unrealistic and unfair to the kids. Either they were part of our family or they weren't. It didn't serve them at all to prevent them from doing things, to treat them as being half-in, half-out. Greyson and Tristan needed stability in their home lives, whatever their future would be. Luckily, the courts sided with us and allowed for the trip.

The six of us drove out to the Outer Banks and spent the week with Reece's parents, sister, niece, and nephew. We rented a house on the shore, and the kids all frolicked and played on the beach. It was the first trip to the beach for Amaya, Makai, Greyson, and Tristan. The three older kids loved it, but Tristan refused to put his feet in the sand. Realizing it wasn't going to happen, Reece bought a blow-up pool and placed it on the beach for him. Seeing my kids building sandcastles with their cousins, going to amusement parks with Mema and Papa, and eating Popsicles and laughing was one of the most satisfying experiences of my life, the realization of what I had always wanted.

When we got back home, no one wanted Greyson and Tristan to leave. Amaya was on the couch crying, saying she wanted them to stay. Reece and I agreed. "Sure, come get their stuff," their foster mother said when I called. All she wanted to know was that she wasn't going to have to return that month's stipend. Through gritted teeth, I told her that wasn't going to happen. She hesitated, so I reassured her that even if the district made her pay it back, we would personally give her the money. We just wanted the boys.

Later that day we drove out to her house in Maryland, and she handed us Greyson's and Tristan's stuff. In two trash bags. It was Amaya and Makai all over again. They had nothing in those bags. Tristan didn't have a bear or blanket or anything. It broke my heart; the boys already had things at our house that we kept for the weekends, but Sunday night to Friday they had so little. I didn't even want to think about it.

•

All of a sudden our home didn't feel so big. With six of us now, the transition was exciting but chaotic. We put Tristan in a crib in our master bedroom. Amaya, who was almost five, switched rooms so she would have her own, since the district would no longer allow her to share a room with the boys. The walls of that room were green because Makai was obsessed with frogs, so Reece went to work. He painted her walls to make them fairy striped, with pink, green, and purple. I was almost jealous of how deft and skillful he was at decorating the rooms.

Greyson and Makai would share Amaya's old room, and we put two separate beds in there. Reece painted zoo animals on the walls, and Greyson put his stuffed cheetah on a shelf, beginning a zoo that would expand fairly quickly.

As expected, our lives were completely upended. But it didn't matter that toys and stuffed animals were everywhere, that the kitchen sink was overflowing with dishes, or that there were millions of sneakers and mud in the hallway. This was what we had asked for—what we had wanted—so we had to sink or swim. Though Reece and I always kept an immaculate home, and both of us liked things in their place, all that went out the window. It had to. Reece was surprised that I was at ease with it, and I was surprised that he was. It was funny how quickly we adjusted. I'd come home to Legos all over the floor and snacks in strange places, and it didn't bother me—we lived in a home, not a museum.

We went from beautiful china to rainbow paper plates, from cocktail parties to curling up on the couch, from staying out late to nightly baths. I loved every minute of it—watching movies that

I hadn't seen since I was little, learning the ins and outs of Wonder Pets and Dora, embracing all the things that hadn't existed in our lives until the kids arrived. It was a transformation, meshing six lives together like that. As expected, there were choppy moments, but we were prepared. We all just held on to each other tight and rode the waves.

· 11 ·

OUT

1990

My mom—Sue—didn't know I was gay. *Nobody* knew—because I never talked about it. Though I had been dating men for years, I had always kept that life hidden, tucked away and wrapped tight. When my mom thought I was going out with some girl, my date was actually with some guy. "Out to a bar" meant a gay bar. She was a Mormon, and though she was less devoted than she used to be, I was afraid she'd never accept me for who I was.

I was also embarrassed, worried about how people were going to treat me. I was twenty-three and my sexual orientation seemed just one more nail in the coffin: abused, uneducated, a product of the system, and gay. By this point I was also working in the banking industry, a notoriously good-old-boy world. I'd hear people make gay jokes or say homophobic slurs around the office and keep my mouth shut. Sometimes I even chimed in.

My biological father, my stepfather, my foster father, my cousins, and my half brothers were all homophobic. Growing up, I didn't know any gay people—at least, no one who would admit to it. Even the older boys I would mess around with never called themselves gay. Before *Will & Grace*, before *Ellen*, the only thing people talked about regarding homosexuality was HIV, which was this "cancer" that was supposedly our punishment.

Late one night I came home from a bar after having gotten into a fight with a guy I was dating. I was sitting on Sue's front porch, smoking a cigarette. Nancy, who was around thirteen, came outside. She stood there quietly for a minute as we both stared out into the dark, my smoke curling into the still night.

"When are you going to tell Mom?" she said.

"What?" I said, almost shocked by her voice. It had been so quiet, and I had been lost in my head. "Tell her what?"

"Terry . . . come on. I know. You don't have to—"

"What are you talking about?"

Nancy was mature for her age. She did this exasperated exhale like I was being a child. "When are you going to tell Mom that you're gay?"

I played dumb for a little longer, but she wasn't buying it and I just didn't have the energy. Then I broke down crying. "Mom will hate me," I said. "I know she's gonna hate me."

"She's not going to hate you, Terry," Nancy said, coming to sit right next to me. "She loves you." So I went upstairs and knocked on my mother's bedroom door, waking her up. "Mom, I need to talk to you," I said into the darkness.

"Terry, what are you . . . It's one o'clock in the morning."

"I have to talk to you," I said. I was nervous, terrified really, but trying to push myself through because I felt like I'd lose my nerve if I waited until morning.

She sat up and turned on the bedside lamp. "Are you okay? What's wrong?"

"I'm gay."

She squinted by the light. "What?"

"I'm gay," I said again. It almost felt good to say it aloud.

A silence. My heart was sprinting in my chest.

"Are you sure?" she asked.

"Yes." It was likely the only sure thing in my entire life.

"Come here," she said, making room for me on the bed. Just like I was a little kid, I crawled into bed with my mom. She shut out the light and I could hear she was crying, which was so painful to me in that moment. It sounded like rejection, and I told her so.

"No, no, Terry. I'm not crying because you're gay," she said. "I'm crying because I know how bad you want to be a dad. And now that's never going to happen."

•

When I was a teenager, I'd resented how much Sue and Eddie made me watch their kids. I could never be free because Nancy, Steven, and Blake were always tagging along, like extra appendages I had to bring everywhere.

But that was the very experience that made me want to be a dad. Part of me had actually loved the need and the responsibility of watching my siblings, loved people depending on me, loved providing what others couldn't and the connection that resulted.

That longing reemerged when I was an adult. I wanted to feel connected again. It was a fierce desire for how my life was supposed to be: I was meant to be a dad. I was also young and naïve enough to believe that being a dad could magically right all the wrongs.

But I couldn't be a dad, because I was gay. That reality wasn't even something anyone questioned.

The night I told my mom that I was gay, she also said, more than once, "Let's not tell Eddie." Though they were separated, he was still coming over every weekend and still had a hold on her. She worried that Eddie would give me a hard time, especially about me being around his sons. It made me sick—*he* was the problem—but I agreed to not say a word.

Anytime Eddie came to the house, he and I wouldn't really talk. The truth—that he had beaten me, thrown me out, and made me homeless—was an elephant in the room. As long as we didn't speak about it, he didn't have to accept what he'd done. And my mother didn't have to acknowledge it. Everyone could just pretend it wasn't there.

One Saturday evening, I was at the kitchen sink doing the dishes after dinner when Eddie walked in and said, "When were you gonna tell me?" That question was the most he had said to me in years.

"Tell you what?" I said, not even turning around.

"When were you gonna tell me that you're gay?"

"What are you talking about?" I faced him, truly surprised. I played dumb; not telling Eddie was something my mother regularly brought up to me.

"I know. I know," he said, a greasy smile on his face. "You know what? It's okay. But I only have one question for you."

"What's that?"

Then he put his arm around me and made a joke too disgusting to repeat.

Sue's family, however, could not have been more supportive. She sat her parents down and was direct. "Terry is my son," she told them, "and he is gay and I love him."

They didn't need any time to come around. "Anyone who disrespects you or has a problem with this," my grandparents said, "is not welcome in our home. You're our grandson and we love you." That unconditional love and acceptance were what I'd always wanted, from the time I was a little boy. My aunts and uncles, all very devoted Mormons, had the same reaction. I was grateful and more than a little surprised, which taught me something: when you open yourself up, you allow things like that to happen. You give people a chance to surprise you. I always try to remember that.

My whole life, I had been too stuck on the idea that what united a family was blood. It had been this irritating fact, a truth that blocked me from feeling a part of something. Blood had always been nothing but a burden to me. But after Sue and her family showed me unconditional love, that perception was fully shattered. I finally saw that family was about how you felt about others. Family was about what you meant *emotionally* to someone, not biologically.

But even though my family showed me love, there remained this glaring missing piece. No one talked about what had happened to me in the four years that I was gone—how Eddie threw me out, how my mom had let him, what I had to do to survive on the streets. When I returned, it was like those years had never happened.

The entire family tended to pretend or glide over painful truths that were plain on our faces. No aunts or uncles ever questioned my disappearance and return, like I had never left. I found out later that Sue had told them all I had run away and she didn't know where I was. Years later, one aunt finally sat me down and asked, "What happened to you? Where did you go?"

I didn't even know where to begin.

•

Coming out to Sue and the family was one weight off my shoulders. I started bringing guys home and introducing them to my family. But I was still in the closet at work, still playing that double role. Because I was trying to climb the corporate ladder, the last thing I needed was an added strike against me.

And even though I was gaining a sense of self, even a little confidence, I was still a troubled kid. The ideas of love and affection and neglect and abuse were all mixed up and tied together. I was constantly lying to myself or to others, getting into fights, falling into hard drugs, and engaging in other risky behaviors. When others treat you like nothing for so long, you start to treat yourself that way.

Enter Jacob. Jacob was like a movie star, tall with blue eyes and blond hair. He was a good deal older than me, in his thirties, and extremely popular in the Baltimore bar scene. When he walked into a room, he demanded everyone's attention and they gave it to him. When he took an interest in me, I was flattered. Dating Jacob was my first relationship in the open, and it made me feel important.

One night I was hanging out at a loud bar we used to frequent, and a friend came and sat next to me. He leaned in to my ear. "Have you seen Jacob?"

I mentioned that he had been outside last I saw him.

"You think he has a quarter?" he asked.

I was confused. "I probably have a quarter," I said, reaching into my front pocket.

He playfully hit me on the back. "You're a riot, Rob."

I was confused as he walked away. When he spotted Jacob, he gestured to him and they moved to the bathroom.

I'd had absolutely no idea that Jacob was a drug dealer, but as became my habit with men, I adjusted to his world. As we started dating, I became part of his orbit, and using things like cocaine was just something we did. Drugs are a mechanism to bury yourself, and that's what I was still doing. Hiding was the most obvious reaction to the life I had lived and the way that I felt. I was destructive enough to feel that drinking heavily and using drugs were the only rational choices.

When Jacob asked me to move in with him, I did, more quickly than I should have. Once we shared a roof, drug use became part of my daily life, as much as showering and going to work. Drugs numbed me to the pain of my life, of how Jacob treated me, of how he made me feel I *deserved* to be treated. He openly cheated on me and sometimes flipped into these rages during which he'd beat me up. And I always allowed it, just like with all the male figures in my life. I didn't want to push against him for fear of setting him off further or, even worse, being rejected.

After one too many of these episodes, I took some stock of myself. I called up my mom, who had been pushing me to leave him for a while. She and Eddie showed up with a truck and helped me pack all my stuff. But I didn't go home—I just moved in with another guy.

While I was dating Jacob, I'd met Scott, who was like Jacob's reverse image. He was gentle and kind, with long, flowing hair and a steady business. I moved in with Scott, but it just couldn't work. I wasn't ready for someone like him, someone who was good. I doubted I deserved his kindness, so I convinced myself it was a lie. A man actually caring about me was such a foreign idea that I rejected it. I attacked him like a virus. I lashed out, constantly accusing him of cheating, freaking out every time he talked to another guy. On top of that, I was drinking too much and still using drugs, which exacerbated my paranoia into a tumbling downward spiral. Until one particular night I went overboard.

After getting smashed at a bar and searching to go lower, I wandered into the back alley, where I found someone with heroin and shot up for the very first time. I hadn't yet crossed that barrier, but in that moment, it felt like the next natural step. So I took it.

I remember flashes after that—a broken needle in my arm, my mother and Nancy showing up outside the bar. Swirling police lights and a crackling radio, blood on my knuckles and shirt, and my mother talking calmly to an annoyed police officer. "Officer, I'm going to take him right to the hospital," she kept saying. The cop was explaining that I had beaten someone up earlier in the night. I did remember that—he had been talking to Scott and I was a jealous wreck. That explained all the blood.

My mom took me directly to the hospital, and when the nurses were out of the room, I ripped all the monitoring equipment off my chest and arm and snuck out, hiding in the back of my mom's car in the parking lot until Nancy found me. I woke up the next morning on my mother's couch with her and Eddie standing over me.

"We're talking, Terry. Right now," my mom said.

Like a child, I put the pillow over my head and groaned. I didn't want to hear it. Not ever, but especially not then.

"No, right now, Terry."

"Terry!" Eddie shouted. "Sit up. Now."

"You have two choices," she said. She wasn't angry, just exhausted and direct. "You can check yourself into rehab right now—"

"Mom, I don't need—"

"Or I will go to court and tell the judge you can't make your own decisions and have you committed and you will stay there. I will do it."

I knew she was telling the truth. Even in the blaring early light. Even through the cobwebs in my brain. So I gave in. That morning they drove me to Howard County General Hospital, where I voluntarily checked myself in to the psychiatric unit.

In the thirty-day program of rehab and psychiatric care, we did AA and NA meetings, group talks, and therapy sessions about our issues. I was only so receptive; I never thought I had an alcohol or drug problem—I had a coping-with-life problem. But just being away from my old haunts and crowd, separate from that circuit, helped me reset. When I got out, I never went back to Baltimore, never saw Jacob or Scott again.

Though I had lost my job, when I left the hospital I came out feeling better about myself. Part of it was being away from my old triggers and habits, and part of it was just, at twenty-five, taking control of *something*. I'm certain I'd be dead today if my mother hadn't intervened. To this day, I feel like I owe her an enormous debt for that alone.

I moved back in to her basement in Maryland and got another job, this time in the mortgage industry. But it wasn't too long before I just replaced one scene with another. I found myself pretty quickly immersed in the DC late-night scene, still drinking, still using drugs. Things can only change so much when you don't change yourself.

I met Mike at a club in downtown DC. He was a handsome man, masculine and preppy. I fell for him so hard that I slipped back into old patterns. He was abusive and demeaning, but I didn't know any other kind of love. I thought that was how it was supposed to be.

Mike's whole life was a lie. He was separated from his wife and so closeted that he lived a double life. No one in his family knew that he was gay, and I was part of his secret, something to remain hidden. When we moved in together, I was never allowed to meet his parents or invited over for the holidays. His mother would leave these disgusting homophobic messages on our machine. That was the extent of my interaction with them. That part of his life didn't exist to me.

My relationship with Mike was toxic. He cheated on me, verbally abused me, and physically attacked me, but I just didn't have the self-esteem to get out from under it. I was a broken kid and he broke me even more. Though I had no connection to Mike's family, my family opened their arms to him and he became one of their own. He gave jobs to all three of my younger siblings, became particularly close to my sister Nancy, and would regularly talk to my mother on the phone.

My family's opinion of Mike was clouded by the way he framed everything. After Mike once left me with a black eye, my mother asked me, "Well, what did you do to make him so mad?" Their common reaction to our problems was that they were my fault. And I'm sure I internalized that. *I deserve it*, I thought. *I must deserve all of it*.

Years of this made it even harder to dislodge myself from what we had built. Thinking back on it, though, I hadn't built it at all. It had just settled into place because I wasn't strong enough to fight it.

I had dug a hole for myself, and with each passing year it got deeper. There was no sense of light, no feeling that I would ever crawl out. I became hopeless about ever finding true happiness, about ever being part of a real family. Until, twelve years into my relationship with Mike, a gift from a friend set me free.

· 12 ·

UNION

2009

With six of us living in the house, routine became our lifeline. A typical day would start around 5:30 a.m. when we'd hear Tristan stirring in his crib in our bedroom. Reece would often get Tristan and bring him into bed. "I'm here, Bubby," Reece would say. Then he would go downstairs to make coffee and fix a bottle while I tickled Tristan's tummy and cooed at him or watched in awe as he slowly woke up.

When Reece came back with Tristan's bottle and my coffee, he'd change Tristan's diaper and get him dressed. Makai or Greyson would loudly get up and often push open their sister's door, waking Amaya, who's a slower riser.

"Let your sister sleep," I'd say, and try to entice Makai and Greyson to unleash their energy in our room, which they would. They'd run in and hop on the bed and start jumping. Makai wasn't talking yet, but he did a lot of pointing and made noises, while Greyson talked a mile a minute—about the breakfast he wanted, about something that happened in day care, about some book we were reading last night. The boys had already developed a tight bond, and Greyson was so protective of Makai. Watching them reminded me of those safe moments with my oldest sister, Fran, and the way I felt protected when she was in charge—how it felt like no matter what my parents did or tried to do, Fran would make sure I was okay.

Reece and I were trying to encourage Makai to use words, so when he would point, we would say, "You want the sippy cup? Sippy cup." or "That's your toothbrush, Makai. Toothbrush."

At first, when Makai would point, Greyson would just get what his brother needed. But he caught on quickly that this was how we were teaching him. Then he would do the same thing—saying the words and trying to get Makai to repeat them. Greyson was so helpful that we called him "A-Plus Boy" or just "A" for short.

He and Makai would bounce up and down on the bed, tossing the covers, trying to touch the ceiling, falling down and giggling like crazy.

After getting dressed, I'd walk down the hall to Amaya's room and wake her up slowly—I'd try to get her excited about breakfast or the school day or something we had planned. She'd put the pillow over her head and roll over or groan like a sleepy teenager though she was only five. Maybe I'd carry her down to the kitchen as she woke, passing the boys on the stairs. Makai had no muscle mass and suffered tibia trauma, so his legs buckled when he walked; it was easier for him to go downstairs backward—with assistance— and Greyson would always help him. Makai sometimes tried to get me to pick him up, but I wouldn't—walking on his own was the only way for him to strengthen his legs. Sometimes he'd throw a fit about it, which was hard to watch, even harder because I knew I could stop it. Other times, especially with Greyson's encouragement, Makai would be okay. It depended on the day and his mood.

Then all the kids would loudly take over the kitchen, pushing and playing, like they'd been siblings forever. Around the table, they sat in booster seats, and Reece would set Tristan up in his high chair. Amaya would help Tristan eat by breaking his food into little pieces. Tristan did not like baby food, so Reece began to cut whatever we were eating and put it on his tray. He ate it, so that's what we began to give him for meals.

One of us would take Amaya to school and the other would take the boys to day care and then we'd both be off to work: me at a mortgage company and Reece as an interior designer. On Reece's lunch break, he'd go over to the day care to see the boys but mostly to check on Makai, who had already been thrown out of three different day care centers. It was frustrating to hear the reports that he was a "bad kid" when we just knew it was a developmental issue no one would address.

At night Reece would make spaghetti for everyone or prepare sides to go with whatever he had put in the Crock-Pot that morning. While he cooked, with Tristan in the high chair eating puffs and Greyson and Makai playing with Wonder Pets, I would help Amaya with her letters or numbers.

Amaya had been going to a preschool that was too overcrowded and understaffed, a place that wasn't teaching her anything. Reece and I took Amaya through the extensive interview process to send her to a top charter school for kindergarten. The school was progressive and art based, and though she was a little behind academically, she got in. We knew she would thrive in a place that was open to a variety of learning styles and that appreciated the diversity in the kids, teachers, and parents. We wanted to expose her to different worlds, to show her that there were a lot of kids living in what society would deem "nontraditional" homes.

After dinner, we'd often take the dogs for a family walk and then have bath time. All three of the boys could bathe together, which made it easier. Every night, without fail, I'd overfill the tub with bubbles, but not because I liked bubbles. Because I was so self-conscious.

Social workers were allowed to come by unannounced, and because we had boys and we were gay, and because Amaya was a girl and we were men, I wanted to keep the kids covered at all times. As their father, the impulse seems ridiculous, but at the time I felt so watched, so judged on every little thing. I didn't want to be misunderstood or give any reason for the district to take the kids away. The process was an exhausting dance that I kept up for far longer than necessary.

Then we'd get the kids into pajamas and all jump in our bed or cuddle downstairs on the couch for reading time. Greyson and Amaya would rotate choosing books and then we'd read to them while Tristan drank from his bottle. Then it was off to bed.

Reece and I tried to make time for each other, to talk about our day or just connect, but more often than not, we'd collapse on the bed or in front of the TV. Luckily, none of the children had any sleep issues. If they had, I'm not sure we would have made it.

•

In the summer of 2009, when Greyson and Tristan had been with us for about two months and Amaya and Makai for six, a pattern began to develop with Nora, Amaya and Makai's mother. For weeks at a time, she'd fail to show up for weekly visitations with the children. Then she'd start coming again, but the visits would be spotty. Sometimes we'd get a phone call ten minutes beforehand that she had cancelled. Or we'd get to the community center, and she wouldn't show up at all. I would sit down with Amaya and Makai, explain that their mother couldn't see them that week, and just try to cheer them up any way I could. There was a lot of ice cream involved.

Reece and I first tried to solve the problem by leaning into it, figuring out ways that we could accommodate Nora. Thinking it might be good if the visits were more regular and outside that one bureaucratic room, we got the courts to approve us to be monitors so we could get in visits on the weekends. After going through the process to do this, Nora only came to one of those weekend visits. And she was checked out the whole time, talking to her boyfriend on her phone. We moved the schedules around, over and over again, but she almost never showed up. On some visitations, Nora would bring Amaya a gift and bring nothing for Makai, or barely acknowledge her son at all, which was so upsetting. She was more like a sister than a mother to Amaya, which just reminded me how young Nora was.

Nora reminded me a great deal of my biological mother, a woman I had grown to forgive as I got older and became a father. I thought about the mistakes she, too, had made, choosing men over her kids, neglecting her children—so many of the same things I was seeing Nora do. The cycle remained in place. Things didn't change.

We made a few attempts to reach out to Amaya's and Makai's other family members—anyone who might want to have a relationship with the kids—and received just one reply. Amaya's paternal grandmother called us back and asked us to bring her over. So we did.

Reece and I drove Amaya to the housing projects where her grandmother lived, and the three of us spent an hour or two there. The dark and damp apartment smelled of marijuana, and there were piles of stuff spilling off tables and out of half-closed closets. There was this sense that many people lived there—though I didn't see anyone else around. The entire time, Amaya's grandmother was distant and didn't really seem that interested in her granddaughter at all. She never called for us to come again.

•

It's hard to admit now, but since I assumed that Amaya and Makai were going back to their mother, I had been a little cautious about opening up to them. A part of me was so scared to let my guard down, worried that a day might come when I would never see them again. I loved them, of course, but I was scared to invest as much as Reece had. I still struggled with this instinct of self-preservation.

But I looked to Reece as a model of how to be with the kids. From day one his heart was wide open to them—it was never about how long they were going to be with us or what might happen when they left. It was about prioritizing what they wanted and what they needed. Watching Reece's interaction with the children, especially Makai, told me this was going to turn out okay, that I didn't have to moderate myself, even that it would be wrong for me to do so.

Reece is far more patient than I am and can juggle so many different things with ease and poise. I've gotten better since we first became parents, but back then I was getting my feet wet: trying to grasp it all, falling in love with them, worrying that they were going to leave, knowing that my financial responsibility was increasing with Reece working less. On top of that, I felt enormous pressure to be perfect. I lived in terror that I was making a mistake, that I was going to be judged, that the district was going to take our kids away because I said or did the wrong thing.

For instance, it took a while for Reece and me to show affection to each other in front of the kids. Most people—especially straight people—might not even think about it, but it was something that weighed heavily on my mind and heart. I didn't want the children to be raised thinking our relationship wasn't normal, but I was also concerned about messages they were receiving outside the home.

Amaya caught on to my reluctance and turned it into a game. A curious girl, she couldn't figure out why we wouldn't hold hands, so she would try to get us to. "Dada, take Daddy's hand," she'd say, trying to link us together. We'd laugh but then end up putting a kid between us. I remember the first time I kissed Reece in front of Amaya; she flashed this thousand-watt smile that just ran through her body. Who doesn't want to see that their parents love each other?

From the beginning of our first parenting class, Reece and I were worried about how to navigate the system with regard to our sexuality and our relationship. Our new social worker, Rich, who took over when we transferred agencies, seemed to do everything he could to make us self-conscious about who we were. His words and actions seemed to shine a spotlight on this.

Every six weeks we'd have a hearing for each pair of kids— one for Amaya and Makai and one for Greyson and Tristan. The hearings were essentially an update from the social worker to the guardian ad litem (the kids' attorney), the parents' attorney, and the judge about how the children were doing. Foster parents generally didn't attend, but we never missed one, just in case the judge needed information from us. (None of the kids' birth parents were usually present.) At one hearing, Rich told the judge he thought it was inappropriate that the kids called us Daddy and Dada, as though that were confusing. He treated the terminology as a problem.

"We didn't ask them to do that," I said. It had actually been Amaya's idea.

One night, a few months prior, Reece and I were getting Amaya ready for bed. Because she was the oldest and we wanted her to have some privileges, we always let her stay up thirty minutes later than her brothers. So she would get this pocket of alone time with me and Reece. After getting Amaya out of the bath and into her pajamas and after a round of Candy Land, we sat down on her bed to read *The Giving Tree* again. I don't think Amaya loved it that much; she just liked that I loved it.

When it was over and I was pulling the blanket up to her chin, she said, almost out of the blue, "I don't want to call you Rob and Reece anymore."

"No, sweetie?" I said.

"What would you like?" Reece asked.

"I want to call you Daddy," she said to me, "and you Dada," she said to Reece.

I turned to Reece and almost lost it right there. I barely held it together.

"Daddy, don't be sad," Amaya said, testing the new word out.

"Oh, Daddy's not sad, honey. Not at all. You just made me the richest guy in the world."

Daddy. I never thought I'd hear those words from a child. Ever.

I flashed back to a day in Sue's kitchen when I was around thirteen. It was late afternoon, the winter light was dimming, and she and I were canning peaches on her kitchen table.

"Can I call you Mom?" I asked her.

"If that makes you feel good, Terry," Sue said, "you better believe you can."

·

To hear the social worker treat Amaya's decision to call us Daddy and Dada as a problem really tore at me. Whether she was ours for a week or forever, she was our daughter and I was responsible to protect her, to guide her, to make her safe. If this little princess wanted to look me in the eye and call me Daddy, who was it hurting?

Cold and judgmental about every little thing, Rich couldn't get past the fact that we were two men. He didn't like that the courts had allowed Tristan to sleep in our room, once asking us, "Isn't that strange having him in the room?" implying that we were having relations with each other with the baby present. Rich ended up quitting and was replaced with another social worker, a lovely woman who truly did have the kids' best interests at heart.

•

When Amaya first had visits with her mother, she would cry when they ended, which was so hard to watch, and it made me feel for both of them. After about a month or so, though, Amaya didn't cry at all; she would skip out to our car with Nora, yell, "Bye, Mommy!" and skip over to us.

When Nora stopped showing up to her visitations, Amaya would ask me, "Where's my mommy?" and in the beginning, I would lie.

"Oh, sorry, honey," I'd say. "Mommy got busy and couldn't make it, but she loves you. She'll see you soon."

It kept happening, though, again and again, and I got angry, mostly because I saw how much it was hurting Amaya. I know that keeping kids in the dark is never the solution. My parents never told me anything, and that fear of the unknown was so much worse than just having to face the situation, no matter how scary.

So I leveled with Amaya.

"Sweetie, Daddy doesn't know why Mommy didn't come," I said. "Sometimes, as a parent, we don't know what to do or what's the right thing. Right now Mommy needs to worry just about Mommy, but you let Daddy and Dada worry about you."

We didn't really speak much of it again. Amaya didn't seem to care about how visiting day kept moving or getting cancelled. Maybe she was building up her own armor or maybe she was actually fine with it. As she got older, we talked more openly about this, but when she was young, I let her decide when to bring it up.

By the fall of that first year with all the kids in the house, the social worker called to say that Nora had entirely dropped out of classes and rehab. Then we got a call that she had moved to Virginia. Four months went by without her seeing the kids at all, even at the mandatory court hearings for her case. Amaya's and Makai's dads were never there—though they weren't required to be—and then Nora simply stopped showing up. The courts offered to pay for her transportation to the visitations and to the court hearings, but she still never showed.

Week after week, our protective instincts for the kids grew stronger and stronger. It was upsetting to see their mother fail them. She had an opportunity to make things right, and the district gave her chance after chance after chance. But that one step forward just never seemed possible.

January 2010

A year after Amaya and Makai had come to us, and about six months after Nora had basically disappeared, the district finally acted. The kids' goal was changed from reunification to reunification/adoption, which is something of an official warning to the birth parents. These were Nora's kids and we were completely supportive of her taking them back if she were able. But we also saw what Amaya and Makai were going through. With heavy hearts, we called a lawyer.

Grandma Calfee didn't watch the kids anymore, but she was still very much in our lives. A sweet soul, she was behind us once she knew we were pursuing adoption. We knew we were doing what was best for Amaya and Makai but also understood the racial optics that would come into play, as did she. Grandma Calfee recommended a well-known lawyer who was a pillar of the African American community. DC was required to give us a court-appointed attorney, though they never did. So we set up a meeting with the lawyer at our home.

Mr. Harris was an African American man in his fifties, tall with glasses. He was a snappy dresser in a long trench coat, bow tie, and fedora hat, and there was a professorial air to him. He spoke in a stern and direct voice that remained at one steady volume. One evening, after the kids' bath time, he came to the house for a meeting, wanting to observe us with the children before agreeing to take the case. He sat quietly in the living room while we conducted our nighttime routine with the children. We were under the microscope once again, which we were used to by now. Under Mr. Harris's watchful eye, we wound the kids down for bedtime, got their teeth brushed, and put them all to sleep. Then Reece and I met with him at the dining room table.

"Okay," Mr. Harris said, as we sat down. He was drinking from a glass of iced tea, the ice cubes clinking around. "So let's start by being up front."

"Of course," Reece said.

"Yes, please," I said. "Be blunt."

"You have very slim chances."

The words just hung there, and my stomach dropped; that was exactly what I'd been afraid he was going to say. But I shook it off and tried not to show my disappointment. Reece and I met eyes.

"Why?" Reece asked, after a long beat.

I knew—I had thought about it all the time—but Mr. Harris answered.

"You are two white, gay men trying to adopt two black kids. And the mother doesn't want it to happen. This is going to be a

fight like you've never fought before," he continued. "But I'm prepared for it. The question is: Are the two of you ready for it?"

"Absolutely," I said. Reece agreed.

I don't know if Mr. Harris realized it, but we had been fighting
for quite some time. This next stage was just a new battle.

For an hour or so, Mr. Harris took notes on seemingly everything in our lives. He asked about our relationship with Amaya and
Makai's mother, Nora, but also about our relationship with Greyson
and Tristan's mother. He inquired into our careers, our friends, our
own childhoods. I told him my history with my parents, how I was
taken into foster care after my mother's death, about being kicked
out of that house at eighteen.

"Tell me about your relationship," he said.

"What do you want to know?" I asked. "We've been together
for three years."

"Is it an open relationship?" he asked.

It was a strange question, one that I knew simply did not get
asked of heterosexual couples. But he was getting ready to fight for
us, so I didn't get worked up about it.

"No," I said.

"Any drugs?" he asked.

"None."

When he was satisfied, I asked if we could ask him some questions. He seemed to like that I was a details guy. "Sure," he said.
"Shoot." I asked him what type of cases he had, what his history

was, if he had any gay friends ("Of course," he said), and about his own personal situation. He told me he had a white girlfriend and no children.

I trusted him implicitly. He didn't pussyfoot at all, which I liked; Reece and I had no interest in being coddled. We wanted to win. By the end of our talk, I was ready to put my entire heart—my family—in this man's hands.

At the end of the conversation, Mr. Harris agreed to take the case. Then he dropped the bomb on us about how much it was going to cost. We might have flinched, but we never hesitated. We ended up taking out a second mortgage, but we refused to be deterred by something as cold as money. In fact, the amount of money he cost told us that he was the best. We were gay, white men with a history of conflict with DC Child and Family Services looking to adopt two African American children. We needed the best.

●

Immediately after we filed for adoption, Amaya and Makai's great-grandmother, Mrs. Toland, filed for adoption as well. Amaya and Makai had been with us for a year, so we wondered why she hadn't petitioned to have them from the very beginning. Mrs. Toland had come to some of the hearings but never spoke to Reece or me—not a word. She clearly didn't want anything to do with us.

Even though she was older—in her sixties at the time with failing health and on dialysis three days a week—and in a house that had been inspected and deemed unsuitable for the children, she was still going to fight us for custody.

I told Mr. Harris I wanted to sit down and have a meeting—a mediation—with Mrs. Toland. "You know as well as we do that she's not fit to raise these two kids," I told him. Mr. Harris got in touch with her attorney, and she agreed to meet with us.

On a rainy morning, we met at Mrs. Toland's lawyer's office in DC, a cold white building with stone-faced people entering and exiting bland conference rooms. Reece, Mr. Harris, and I waited inside one at a long wood table, drinking coffee out of foam cups and watching raindrops smack the large windows. After some time, in walked a pear-shaped lawyer, disheveled and with glasses falling off the tip of his nose—the comical opposite of Mr. Harris.

Behind him was Mrs. Toland, moving slowly, in a long trench coat.

Mrs. Toland was Nora's maternal grandmother and had raised her (Nora's mother had died some time ago). She was a devoted Baptist with long fingernails and kind eyes. And now she was seated across from two gay men who wanted to adopt her great-grandchildren.

We laid it all out for Mrs. Toland: how we loved Amaya and Makai like they were our own, how we only wanted what was best for them, how we didn't want them to grow up in the system. She agreed with us that Nora just simply had not done anything to help her kids and that it was important somebody capable stepped in.

It was clear from our talk that the Toland heritage, and making sure the kids knew they were Tolands, was part of her calculation. We promised her that this was important to us, too, and that we would not keep her away from the kids. She could be part of the kids' lives in any way she wanted. We explained that we would never move without her knowing where we were, and that our door was always open. We wanted to build a relationship with her—maybe one day with Nora, too.

By the end of that two-hour meeting, the walls around Mrs. Toland had completely crumbled. She opened up to us, talked freely about how she had tried with Nora but couldn't get her to see what the kids needed, and about the difficulties with her other children and grandchildren. She wanted the best for Amaya and Makai but not without them knowing that they belonged to a long line of Tolands. We looked her in the eye and promised her, "These children will know where they came from. You never have to worry about that."

At the end of the meeting, we all hugged, and I could literally feel a path opening up. Not just one to Reece and me, though I felt that, too. It was a path that linked Mrs. Toland with her great-grandchildren.

Because of the way I grew up, I never wanted any connection to my past. Everything back there just felt like pain, like something to be buried or swept away. But I hoped it could be different for my children; I wanted them to understand their heritage and have pride in where they came from.

We got a call the next day that Mrs. Toland had withdrawn her adoption petition.

Soon after, she said we should call her Grandma Toland, since everyone else did. From that moment on, we were family. We'd have pizza dinners at Ledo's, laugh and tell stories, and get together for holidays. She never does for any of the children without doing for all four. Even though Greyson and Tristan aren't related to her, she still treats them as grandchildren.

The outcome was all Reece and I wanted—to keep the kids connected to who they were and who loved them. Because of Grandma Toland, we get to tell Amaya about when she was a baby and she used to follow her great-grandfather around his garden, and my children remain connected to their history. I can share with Amaya and Makai the stories Grandma Toland told us about what it was like growing up in Southern Virginia and about the small all-black school she went to. Because of Grandma Toland, my children will have a fuller sense of themselves, and with her and Mr. Harris on our team, we were one step closer to our future.

· 13 ·

RODGER'S GIFT

1991

Throughout my time with Mike, I carried this heavy longing: I wanted a family. As a child, teenager, and then young man, I had dreamed and yearned for one. A family was all I ever wanted, and during my twelve years with Mike, the possibility was kept locked away from me. Not only did Mike not want kids, he put up these walls blocking me off from his own family, and there was nothing I could do about it. My life had always felt unmistakably incomplete; at the center was this hole.

After Mike and I moved in together, I met a soft-spoken and elderly African American gentleman named Rodger, who lived across the street from us. He was confident, well mannered, and conservatively dressed. Retired from his government job and just barely getting by, he was doing things like baking cakes to pay for his electricity bill. Rodger was stubborn and ornery at times but loving underneath.

"I'll tell you something," he said to me once.

"What's that?"

"I don't need another friend."

"No?"

"Certainly not a white friend," he said, smiling.

Eventually our friendship became something like a father-son relationship, though that description went both ways—we each provided what the other needed. There were such wide gaps in my relationship with Mike that I needed someone to fill that part of me. And Rodger didn't have any family of his own, so we fed each other's needs.

We would play cards and talk about cooking and baking, which he loved. He would tell me stories about his life, which he'd lived entirely in DC, about growing up with a single mom who worked as a housekeeper. He said that when he was young, black people weren't allowed on the beach, and when he went to visit his mom at her job with a white family, she would sneak him out onto the beach at night so he could touch his feet to the sand.

Rodger—whom I started to call Pops—loved me uncondi-tionally, even on bad days and through my poor choices, and he became part of my family. When Rodger met my grandparents—Sue's parents—they opened up their arms to him and he to them.

Rodger was getting up there in years and his health wasn't great, so when Mike and I moved out of DC to a house in Virginia, it only made sense that I would invite Rodger to come live with us.

"Are you kidding?" Mike said when I proposed it. "Come on, Rob. You don't have to do that."

"I know I don't have to. I want to. It's what you're supposed to do."

Mike knew I wasn't going to just let Rodger go, so he gave in.

Rodger had never lived outside the city, but he knew it was time. I invited him to come live with us and told him to keep his monthly social security check and spend it on what he wanted. He helped us pick out the house because it was important to me that he had that feeling of home. I bought him his first new car, a red Lincoln Town Car, which he kept immaculate, and took him on a cruise to the Caribbean.

It was so natural to want to take care of Rodger, because he took care of me. And I wanted to be wanted. I loved being needed. Helping someone find happiness moved me in a way that nothing else could. Rodger was such a giving person that even when his health declined further, he'd drive into DC daily to feed a friend of his who was in a wheelchair. That was just the kind of person he was.

2002

About eight years into our time living together, Rodger got congestive heart failure. I took time off from work to take care of him and stay with him. There was no way on earth I was going to let him die anywhere else than at home with someone who loved him. We brought in a hospice nurse four days a week and tried to make him as comfortable as possible. As his condition worsened, I was afraid to even leave the house, afraid I'd return and he'd be gone. He accepted what was happening, and I respected him too much to pretend any other way. We just vowed to treat every day like it could be his last.

One quiet afternoon, the day's light streaming through the open window, Rodger turned to me. "You know I'm gonna die," he said in almost a whisper. "I just want you to be happy."

"I know," I said.

"Please promise me that you'll make sure you're happy."

"Okay. I will," I said, struggling not to cry. His love for me carried such grace and kindness. It made me feel human after years of not feeling that way at all.

"You need to leave Mike," he went on. "You need to leave him and get on with your life." Rodger had known how miserable I was in that relationship, how unhealthy it was, how it was eating away at me from the inside. "You may find someone else, or you may not," he said, "but you have to try. Try to fulfill everything you want in life."

"Okay, Pops. Okay. You have my word."

"It's okay to take," Rodger had said to me more than once. "You always give but you never take. You've *got* to be able to take." He was right.

By his bedside, in his final days, I took Rodger's hand and asked, "What do you want? What can I do for you?"

He turned his head toward me and smiled weakly. His answer was immediate, like he'd been carrying it forever: "I want to put my feet in the sand."

The next morning, I put Rodger into the car and we drove the three hours to Virginia Beach. When we got there, I wheeled him onto the sand and we sat there together for a few hours, watching the waves and listening to the gulls. "When I'm gone," he said, "I'd like you to sprinkle my ashes on the beach."

I nodded, though even then, I knew I'd have trouble parting with him.

A few mornings later, I could see that Rodger wasn't going to make it through the day. I put Etta James, his favorite singer, on the bedroom stereo and opened up the windows and shades to let the light and air in. "It's okay, Pops," I said. "I'm ready. It's okay for you to let go."

His eyes found mine. "I love you," he said in a weak voice. And then he took his last breath in my arms.

I cried for some time and heard my grandparents come in downstairs. I went down and asked them to call the funeral home and then went back upstairs to be with Rodger. I cleaned him up in the basin tub, dressed him in clean pajamas, and spent some quiet time alone there with him.

I had never lost anyone I'd loved so much. My biological mother's death unmoored me, but we were never close. I didn't miss her beyond being scared of being left alone with Frank. And my biological father's death came as a relief. The grief of losing Rodger hurt as bad as anything I'd ever felt, like a physical pain running through my body. Rodger had brought so much light into my life at a time when I needed it to survive. He confirmed something that I had always thought: just because the same blood doesn't run in our veins doesn't mean we're not family. Rodger made that true in my heart.

Throughout the weeks after, as I mourned for Rodger, as I tried to stay grateful that he had been a part of my life at all, there was this other heavy concern pressing on me: I'd made a promise to Rodger about what I was going to do with my life, and I was going to keep it.

I'd always been a creature of routine and habit, holding for dear life onto even self-destructive things. I had stayed with Mike for so long out of fear—fear of the unknown, fear of upsetting others, fear of being alone. My world revolved around him in a way that made it hard to imagine any other life.

Once Rodger was gone, there was an emptiness that filled every room. It was the same house where I'd lived for years, but now I was completely lost. In spirit, Rodger stayed with me, constantly reinforcing that I was a good person and didn't deserve to be treated the way Mike treated me.

Everyone else thought I was falling apart, but on the inside, I was lying low and getting stronger. I made a vow: no more. No more being the victim, no more being controlled by someone, no more putting my life in someone else's hands. No more staying with Mike to make my mother and siblings happy, to keep my brothers in a job, to not rock the boat. I had been sacrificing for everyone else, neglecting myself in the process. I knew a storm would come the moment I broke away; the only question was how to weather it.

About a month after Rodger died, Mike came home from work, and I met him downstairs in the kitchen, where he was standing up against the island, going through some papers. I looked at him and said, "I have to end this relationship."

"What?" he said, barely paying attention.

"I want to end this relationship," I said. "I have to."

Mike looked up, as though hearing me for the first time. "What are you talking about, Rob?"

"You don't want kids and I do," I said, nervously running the words together. My breath was shallow, but I kept going. "And if I don't leave you now, I will never leave you. And I have to have kids in my life. I have to be a dad."

"You're crazy. You're not—"

"Mike!" I said, raising my voice. "Listen to me. We're over. I am done with this."

My tone lit a fuse in Mike, and he just started going off, screaming at me. "You're not fucking leaving me! You're not fucking going anywhere, Rob." His reaction was about what I'd expected, which was why I'd prepared in advance. "Where the fuck do you think you're gonna go?!"

I had already taken my money out of our joint account.

"Who the fuck do you think is ever going to take you?" he said, but I just let his words bounce off me. I tried to turn the volume down on that raging voice that once held such power over me, that once made me feel like a small child hiding in the tall grass.

The house was in my name. The credit cards were in my name; all the cars were in my name. Mike didn't really own anything. Legally, it was all mine.

I already had my bags packed. "I'm going away," I said. "When I get back, I want you gone." Then I walked out the front door.

I got in my car, pulled down the street, and called my mom: "I left Mike," I told her, "and I'm going on vacation."

"What?"

"I don't want to hear what you think, Mom. I left him and I'm going away."

"Terry, I don't understand. Where are you going?"

"I don't know."

"Well, can you tell me how long you'll be gone?" she asked.

"A week. Maybe two."

"Terry, you have to know where you're going."

"Mom, I don't know," I said. "I'm getting in my car and driving south. Wherever I end up is where I end up. I'm getting on the interstate now. I will keep you posted." And I hung up.

I got on I-95 South and just drove and drove and drove, the country unfurling itself ahead of me, as if just for me. And it felt so good. It felt like lightness, like freedom, like I had finally made a choice for myself. I drove to Savannah, to Fort Lauderdale, to Miami, and then on to Key West, where I had once vacationed with Rodger and Mike. Key West just felt like the right place to go—the last place I could get to on the map. So that's where I started over. I was thirty-five years old and reintroducing myself to the world.

I walked into a town where nobody knew me, nobody knew Mike, Rodger, my family, my baggage. My life had felt like one long intake of breath. Now I just exhaled and heeded Rodger's voice: *It's time for you to take. Take in the air; take time. Take whatever you want.*

Rodger's gift was to set me free. My whole life had been the story of something or someone controlling me. For the first time in my life, I was in charge. It took losing someone I loved to give me the strength to love myself. To become free. To look forward. To take and be okay with taking.

I lived in Key West for a year, working remotely for my job and laying the groundwork to start again. Shattered things can't be glued back together; they have to be rebuilt. So that's what I did.

Key West is the kind of place where I could be anybody I wanted to be. And I found out something: I liked who I was. It was something I had never been able to say.

I returned to DC a year later as a new man, someone who liked himself—and who was ready to truly love someone else.

· 14 ·

TRIALS

March 2010

Life with the children had become normal. Or as normal as life with four young children can be. Bonding with them and watching them grow were welcome and wonderful experiences, the realization of a lifelong dream. Sometimes, I would think back to those times when I was sure I would never be a dad and just be dumbstruck, incredulous, because here we were—together.

We were learning what it was like to be a family, navigating what families have to navigate, sharing and bickering and loving and laughing. We were a family in any and every sense of the word. There was just one thing missing.

In 2008 and 2009, states across the country were coming around and allowing same-sex marriage. Mayor Fenty signed a bill in December of 2009 legalizing same-sex marriage in DC, which was to go into effect in March of 2010.

I don't think the public realized how important it was, not just symbolically but practically. Single-income gay couples all over the country were scared because if, God forbid, something happened to the breadwinner, they couldn't receive any benefits and had no claim on property, life insurance, or anything else. Even hospital visits were an issue for the unmarried.

One Saturday morning, I was sipping my coffee and watching the news when I saw that DC was going to start issuing marriage licenses the next week. I ran up the stairs and found Reece changing Tristan. "Reece!" I said. "They're issuing licenses in DC! Do you want to get married?"

Reece looked up at me, nonplussed. "Are you kidding me?" he said, half laughing. "I'm changing a diaper right now."

"I don't mean *this second.*"

"Oh. Okay," he said. "Let's do it." Then he turned his attention back to Tristan, tickling his belly. "Daddy and Dada are getting married!" I ran off to tell the other children.

That Monday morning, Reece and I were at the courthouse before it even opened, lined up with the other excited couples, trading stories and sharing good wishes. When the doors opened, a communal and celebratory atmosphere filled the air. As the morning rolled on, people would cheer as couples exited. A justice of the peace was even right there in the building, and some couples were getting married on the spot.

We knew we couldn't afford a big wedding, because we were

buried deep in attorney fees and focused on the upcoming trial to adopt Amaya and Makai. We had also just bought a house in suburban Maryland and were in the process of moving out of DC; raising four kids in the city would be too much of a challenge, plus we wanted to get better schooling for Makai. So we planned on a small ceremony with a minister in our new sunroom with about twenty-five family members and friends.

The only day we could get married was a Sunday, a few weeks later, which happened to be Greyson's third birthday. So we had the wedding in the morning and then made all the wedding items disappear for Greyson's party in the afternoon. We felt bad that we were asking him to share the day, but he didn't seem to mind. He actually loved telling people that his birthday was on Daddy and Dada's wedding day. We have photographs of the wedding ceremony and party mixed in with shots of Greyson unwrapping birthday presents. The day was somehow the culmination of everything I had been trying to bring into my life. My love for my husband and for my son are intertwined, eternally linked.

•

Once the wedding was out of the way, we buckled down with Mr. Harris to get ready for court. Preparing for the trial to adopt Amaya and Makai dredged up so many issues we were having with the system. My resentment had built considerably over the years. My experience as a foster child, then of being homeless, then of needing permission to marry, and then of having to go through hoops to get basic help for our children all forged into something hardened.

The process of navigating the foster care system was constant aggravation marked by regular insults. The bureaucracy was so far removed from common sense, so focused on a series of things that simply did not matter: from not being able to take pictures of our foster children to not cutting their hair, to requiring that we all slept on the same floor of our home, to not being able to get them bunk beds.

The bunk bed issue captured so much, in my opinion. In DC— as well as in some other states—foster children cannot sleep in bunk beds because they are viewed as unsafe. Of course, any parent can go out and buy a bunk bed and not think twice about it; it's a treat, something fun for siblings, a bonding tool, and an efficient use of space. It may seem like a small thing, but it's not: if bunk beds were allowed, more children would have homes simply because there would be more room for them. It's just one of the million little examples, but it reveals so much.

Social workers were constantly coming in and out of our brownstone and seemed interested in the most inconsequential things, suffering from a bureaucratic blindness that didn't serve the children—just the rules as they were written. The interactions with them lacked a certain basic humanity.

Of course the district needs to check on the kids, and I know there are unfit foster parents out there. But it should be a *partnership*. From day one, Reece and I always felt looked down upon, like they were waiting for us to drop the ball so they could pounce. We had to deal with completely irrelevant questions when it came to parenting, from every end of the spectrum: our sexuality, our race, even our economic standing, which allowed us to hire private attorneys to fight for things the kids needed.

Even though we were using our money for the children's benefit—to buy them clothes and take them on trips—the district made us feel like we were doing something wrong. They judged us for it. The irony is that so many foster parents were only interested in the money they were getting, whereas we didn't need it at all. We just wanted to be parents.

The fight really began over trying to address the issue with Makai's legs, which were buckled in, making it difficult for him to walk. Why had his medical needs not been addressed? Obviously, he needed to see a specialist, but the social worker was dismissive. She told us to just bring him to the clinic that DC Child and Family Services used, which was wildly understaffed and overcrowded.

We went there once and I refused to go back—it was a nightmare. DC would not let us take him to an orthopedic surgeon, even though we were offering to pay for it. Those restrictions—and the nonsensical reasons behind them—drove us crazy.

The trial for custody of Amaya and Makai was the climax of this nearly two-year battle with the district. Once it began, I woke up every morning with a pit in my stomach, like a hollowness that wouldn't go away. We were teetering, one decision away from our children being taken from us. Just the thought of losing Amaya and Makai after all our time together was too much to bear. As Mr. Harris had warned us, we were headed into an uphill fight; he reminded us that our chances of winning were slim, that the district was unlikely to rule in our favor.

I was also battling my own demons. The legal process triggered a lot for me, and my past felt alive inside that courtroom. After so many years of pushing it down or hiding from it, it bared its teeth and came at me: absent parents, a broken system, regular abuse, kids who were unwanted or uncared for. I carried all the different versions of me, like those Russian nesting dolls: I was a seven-year-old scared of my parents, a twelve-year-old being thrown out by my stepfather, an eighteen-year-old unsure of where I was going to sleep that night. And even when I shook off those memories, the reality wasn't much better: I was a grown man who was in danger of losing two children I loved with all my heart.

We had to convince the court that Nora and each of the kids' fathers were unfit to take Amaya and Makai. Only once the government had terminated the parents' rights could our adoption petition proceed. None of the parents could actually be awarded the children yet. If Reece and I lost the case, Amaya and Makai would stay in foster care. The parents were fighting against our adopting them, in the hopes that one day they could reassert their parental rights. If we lost, Amaya and Makai could spend years in the system, something I wanted them to avoid at all costs. That would be the worst possible result for them, and it was something we simply could not allow to happen.

On the first day of the trial, Reece and I, along with Grandma Toland, entered the small courtroom and sat on one of the two long benches in the back. At the other end of the bench were two men in their midtwenties, one of whom I recognized as Amaya's father. We gave a little wave, and he nodded back. Reece and I had met him a couple of times—every once in a while, he would pop up and want to see Amaya. The other young man was Makai's father, whom we had never laid eyes on. Neither had Makai. Nora was nowhere to be seen.

In front of us all the legal players sat at a long table: Nora's attorney, Amaya's father's attorney, Makai's father's attorney, the attorney for the District of Columbia, a federal attorney, the guardian ad litem, the social worker, and Mr. Harris.

In front of that table was the bench where the presiding judge sat. He was a tall and thin African American man, soft-spoken and distinguished. Since there was no jury, Amaya and Makai's future was entirely in his hands. The very fact that one person held all our cards made me nervous, but after the first day I eased a bit. He seemed trustworthy, nonjudgmental, and wise. I wasn't really worried about him, though. I knew it was going to be the parents' lawyers who were going to try to tear us down.

•

The second day, when Reece and I arrived in court, again with Grandma Toland, we were the only ones on the benches: Amaya's father, Makai's father, and Nora had all not showed.

When it was my turn to go up on the stand, Nora's lawyer, an African American woman with grayish hair and a cold demeanor, went with the full-frontal attack. Though it was her job to be adversarial, it felt like she just didn't like me—from the tone of all her questions to the way she rolled her eyes, to the subtle jabs at who I was as a person.

"RC,"* she asked, "do you think that the courts have done enough to help Nora get her children back?"

"It's not for me to say," I answered.

---

* Throughout the trial, we were never referred to by our names: I was RC (Rob Chasteen), and Reece was MS (Maurice Scheer).

"But we're asking," she said curtly.

"Well, then, I would say . . ." I looked over at Mr. Harris for a signal, but he was poker-faced. "I honestly don't think this is about what the courts are doing. It's what Nora is doing. Or not doing."

"How do you mean?"

"She's making the choices for herself, not her children."

"So their mother is not deserving of help?" she asked.

"That's not what I said," I replied. I was careful not to attack Nora, knowing the judge was likely to be sympathetic to her. But her lawyer was forcing me into a corner. "Look," I said, "the courts have done a lot of bending over backward, offering her transportation and whatever. And so have we—changing the schedules, becoming monitors, offering weekend visits. She just didn't show up."

"Understood." She went over to her spot on the table and picked up some papers. "Have you and your partner unfairly or unduly influenced the social worker to favor you over Nora?"

"Husband."

"Excuse me?"

"Ree— I mean, MS is my husband. Not my partner."

"Sorry—my mistake. Husband." I heard a drop of mockery in her voice, just subtle enough for me to catch. "Did you and your husband unduly influence the social workers?"

"I don't know what that means," I said. "We didn't bias the

social workers, if that's what you're asking. We did what was asked of us." Frustrated, I met Reece's eyes in the back, and he nodded. Just that connection gave me strength. "Well, it was more than that because the kids deserved everything. We did all we could to show we were fit parents. I don't see how that's a bad thing."

"Did you and your husband plan on adopting these kids from the very beginning?" she asked.

"No, not at all," I responded, surprised. "We knew the children's goal was reunification, and we supported that. So we saw our role as providing for the children, protecting the children, until that day came."

"And that day is here," she said.

I didn't reply, and I don't think she expected me to.

"As white men," she said, "do you and MS think there is any way you'll be able to preserve the children's African American heritage?"

I had thought about this quite a bit and knew I couldn't fake my answer. "I can't teach my children how to be black," I said, a statement that I've since made many times. "I'm not going to sit here and tell you or the court that I can do that. All I can do is teach my children how to be good people."

"So you're saying their heritage is not important?"

"No, I didn't say that. We can't do it on our own, but we are going to make sure to have people in our lives to support us who can educate Amaya and Makai on their heritage. We have friends, the kids have teachers, we have Grandma Toland, Grandma Calfee. But I don't see that race has anything to do with this. I'm sorry, but I just don't."

During a recess, Mr. Harris took me aside. "You have to stop that, Rob."

"Stop what?" I asked.

"Stop answering so broadly."

"What does that mean?"

"Just give them a yes or no," he said.

"Why?"

"Because . . . it doesn't help us." He spoke like someone who had done this thousands of times. "It doesn't help you get Amaya and Makai. All it does is open the door to a variety of other issues. We don't want the judge to consider race and sexuality, and we don't want to encourage the lawyers to ask questions about it."

"I'm sorry, but I just don't accept that. I don't," I said, building up anger. Not at Mr. Harris but at the whole process. "What are we afraid of? Let's get it all out there. They have to hear where I'm coming from. Yes and no doesn't tell the judge anything."

•

When we came back from break, I was back on the stand.

"Let's talk about the fact that there would be no mother in the home," Nora's lawyer said. "How are you and MS going to give the support Amaya needs as a young lady, especially as she gets into her teen years, without a mother?"

"There are many children in the world raised by just a father," I said. "Kids who grow up to be good citizens. It has nothing to do with her having no female role model."

"So a girl doesn't need a female role model?"

"I didn't say that," I replied. "Amaya will have lots of female role models, including Grandma Toland, who we have become very close with. And we never said we didn't want Amaya's mother in her life. We never excluded her. What we wanted was for her to take anger management classes, parenting classes, whatever the district determined she needed. And we still don't want to keep her away. As long as she does what's required and doesn't disrespect us, she can come break bread at our table anytime and be part of the children's lives."

Then Mr. Harris stood up. (Mr. Harris had long ago asked us to call him by his first name, but the formal name just suited him.)

"Let me ask you," he began, "why do you and MS want to adopt Amaya and Makai?"

"First of all, I have a bond with them," I said, my voice easing at the topic. "These are two kids who came into our home and our lives who needed us as much as we needed them. I think it's our responsibility to make sure that they have the best they can possibly get in their lives."

He asked about Grandma Toland, how we developed a relationship with her, how she had bonded with our whole family, including Greyson and Tristan. He asked about Greyson's and Tristan's relationship with Amaya and Makai, and I talked about how the siblings were together. Then he asked what our interactions with Nora were like, how we felt when she cancelled visitations or didn't show up.

"Well, those were Nora's choices," I said. "But it hurt us because it was hurting our children."

The attorney for the district asked how we were financially going to be able to support all four children if Greyson and Tristan remained in our home.

"There are lots of families with four kids," I said. "I can't predict what the future will bring for my employment or my husband's employment. All I can say is we're going to do everything we can to support our children and give them the best we can."

While driving home from court at the end of the day, I would just sob. Navigating the legal system, the exhaustion of fighting, the lawyer's insults, the threat looming over our lives: it all almost broke me. The worst part was that if we lost the trial, even if Amaya and Makai weren't going back to their parents, they couldn't stay with us as foster children. The court decided staying with us would be too emotionally painful for them, so they'd be moved to another foster home.

Reece would always remind me of how good we had it, how much love we had, how lucky we were. He'd make sure our day would end on a particular positive note—something the kids had done or said—bringing us back to why we were doing all this. He was a buoy keeping me afloat.

On the last day of the trial, Amaya's father was there again. Nora, who hadn't shown up for a single day, contacted the judge with some convoluted story about why she couldn't make it. He let her call in and listen on speakerphone. We also found out where Makai's father had been: he was in jail, having been arrested on a murder charge.

Nora would not let the proceedings go on without breaking in. She kept talking over the lawyers and the judge, saying she was not agreeing to have Amaya and Makai put up for adoption, that they were her children, that she wanted them back.

Eventually, the judge had enough. "I need you to stop talking over everyone," the judge told her. "You had an opportunity to come to court, and you did not. You're lucky I'm having you on speakerphone. You're to listen in only, please."

Later that day, Amaya's father took the stand. He was medium-sized, in his early twenties, and wearing a T-shirt and jeans. He had rough edges, but he was a thoughtful guy, cordial to Reece and me. We felt nothing but kindness toward him.

As he was being questioned, he started to break down. "I want my daughter," he said, his voice low and cracking. "But I know that I can't have her. And if I can't get her, I know that she is with the best she could be with. I know that Rob and Reece really love

Amaya." As a father, my heart broke for him. He admitted that he couldn't say one bad thing about us and agreed to sign his rights over.

Then it was finished. We all went home and just waited. During the weeks the judge had to make his ruling, we just had to go about our lives, not showing the kids the anguish we were going through, the fear of losing them that we were carrying. I barely kept it together.

Finally, after weeks of not knowing, of flinching every time the phone rang, Mr. Harris called. The judge had made his decision; the ruling would come down in a few days.

The uncertainty made me sick. The morning of the ruling, I was so nervous I threw up before we left the house. The judge was going to look us in the eye and either give custody to us or take the kids away and put them in a new foster home. The district could let their lives drag on in the system for who knew how long. And, if we lost, the social workers would come *that day* to take them away.

We arrived in the courtroom, again with Grandma Toland, who held our hands as the judge read his ruling. We looked around and didn't see Amaya's father or Nora there, but the judge again let her call in on speakerphone. Once the attorneys were all present, the judge read the docket, page after page after page. My heart was in my throat, and I gripped Reece's hand tight.

And I couldn't understand a word.

It was a lot of technical language, legal jargon about termination of parental rights that was way over my head. It was not until the judge finished and inserted his own comments that I knew for sure. "Out of the adoptions I have approved," he said, "I truly believe that this adoption is of the utmost benefit to the children and truly the best outcome for them." We had won.

Reece and I were crying. We got up and hugged everyone: Mr. Harris, the social worker, the DA, the guardian ad litem, Grandma Toland. It was such a special moment.

After two years of loving Amaya and Makai as our own, they were finally our children.

That night we went out to dinner to celebrate and all four of the kids were ecstatic.

We turned the actual signing of the adoption papers into a celebration. The kids dressed up, and we invited all our friends—including Grandma Calfee and Grandma Toland—over to the house. My friend Michelle made cookies with Amaya's and Makai's names and the date to commemorate the occasion. People brought balloons and cake, and we rented a bus to take everyone downtown to the court.

The judge said he'd never seen so many people show up for an adoption signing. The room was so packed that he had to find a bigger court, which we also filled. The message of support being communicated to our children was loud and clear. The kids could look around and know how many people loved them and cared about them. So much about foster care is not feeling loved, not feeling wanted, and not feeling connected to others. It's a life alone.

For Amaya and Makai, that sense of community and family was tied to the day they became ours. Peering around the jam-packed room, I found both of my children, wrapped my arms around them, and held them tight, vowing to never let go.

REECE

February 2005

By my late thirties, I had never been in a relationship that wasn't abusive. Over the years, I had developed confidence in my career, but on a personal basis, I carried serious anxiety and insecurity. Growing a sense of myself, of the space I held in the world, had taken me a long time, but I now knew that no one else could occupy the same spot that I did.

It had been a while since I was last single, though, and after returning to DC from Key West, I took time to enjoy it. My self-esteem had been minimal, and I had spent years beating up on myself. All of a sudden, to find affirming, kind people who found me attractive felt like an ego boost. In the back of my mind, though, it felt fleeting. What I really wanted was to begin a family, to find someone who wanted a home life with kids as much as I did.

One night in the Green Lantern, a gay bar in DC, with my

brother Blake, I watched two men walk in from the winter night. One of them caught my eye, handsome but shy, maybe a little bit younger than me. He had no hair, but he wore a Kangol hat and a stylish leather coat. Both of his ears were pierced with silver hoops.

Everything in the room seemed to stop; the voices were drowned out for a second. Somehow I could just tell that he was a gentle soul—I could feel his calm from across the bar. We looked at each other as he walked past me, and I watched him go up the steps to the upstairs bar, trying to burn a hole into him with my eyes.

"What are you looking at?" Blake asked.

"Who," I said.

"Who?"

"That one." I pointed him out. "I'm gonna date that guy right over there."

"Yeah right, Terry. How about another drink?"

"Nope. Trust me," I said. "I know it."

After a few minutes, I went to the upstairs bar to get another look at him.

The guy's friend noticed me looking and walked over to me. "I see you guys looking at each other," he said. "If you want to talk to him, you are gonna have to walk over there because he's *not* going to come to you."

"Really? Okay." By then I had become the kind of guy who would approach anyone, so I walked over to where he was standing at a high table back by the brick wall.

"Hi, I'm Rob," I said over the music, which was considerably louder upstairs. "What's your name?"

"Maurice," he said.

"What?!" I thought I had misheard him.

"Uh, Maurice," he said. I might have sounded harsh.

"Did you say Maurice?" I asked.

He nodded.

That can't be. There was no way this guy was a Maurice. He didn't look like a Maurice. Not even close. A Chris, maybe. Or a Kevin. Not Maurice. I figured he was putting me on.

"You know," I said, "if you don't want to tell me what your name is . . ."

He pulled out his wallet and showed me his driver's license. Sure enough, his name was Maurice. "Why would I lie about my name?" he asked. I noticed he had a soft voice. Even though he had to speak up over the crowd, it still sounded gentle.

"Okay, I believe you." I laughed. "So what do other people call you?"

"Maurice," he said, exasperated by now.

"Wait—everyone calls you Maurice?"

"Yes. That's my name. Everybody calls me Maurice."

"Well, that's not going to work," I said. "I need to call you something else."

I've always put a great deal of stock in names. They are the way I order the universe. "Maurice" simply didn't fit this man.

"Has anybody ever called you something else?" I asked.

He shrugged. "Well, my nephew and niece can't say my name so they call me Reece."

"That's good. I like that. Reece," I said, feeling the sound of the word. "How about I call you Reece?"

"Fine with me," he said.

We immediately hit it off. Maurice Scheer was in graduate school for interior design while also cutting hair to pay the bills. "Wait," I said. "Your last name is Scheer and you cut hair?"

"Yes," he said, smiling. "A lot of people think it's a fake name."

"Like Maurice," I joked.

"No, that one was just you," he said playfully.

He had an easy way about him; he was inviting and open and made me feel that way as well. I told him a little bit about myself, how I was working in the mortgage business, how I was out with one of my brothers, who was living with me at the time. We agreed to meet for Chinese food the next night, an actual date.

Before the food even came out on our first date, I asked if he was interested in kids.

"Whoa, that's a weird question to ask someone you just met," he said.

"Well, let's not waste each other's time, you know?" I said.

"Okay, then. I do want kids," he said. "Not this second, though. I've put too much time into school not to finish."

This seemed totally reasonable to me. Plus, I was still trying out this new version of myself—so I was willing to wait. For a little while.

I had come to believe that what I wanted was out there. I was determined to keep looking until I found it. And that night, in that bar, it walked right in.

Reece and I didn't start regularly dating right away—we just slowly kept gravitating back toward each other. I'd go out on a date and see Reece and then we'd text each other, or I'd leave a date and call Reece and we'd hang out. I'd go watch TV with him while he studied. The way our relationship evolved was so slow, easy, and natural.

But as I realized I was falling in love with Reece, those emotions became terrifying. Part of the reason was experience—I knew that when you fall in love, the pain starts.

People come into our lives at certain times for a reason. If I had met Reece any earlier, I would have thrown away everything we had built. In fact, I almost did. We went on a vacation to Las Vegas about a year into dating, and on the flight there, and even during the first day, I was planning on breaking up with him. I was still messed up enough that the normalcy, and his kindness, felt abnormal to me. My perception of love and relationships was so confused that the comfort felt uncomfortable.

Then we were sitting across from each other at lunch in some nameless Vegas restaurant, and I was listening to him talk and I just knew. Something clicked. I can't explain it except that it was like this gentle easing. I thought of Rodger and how he had said I deserved to be happy. I thought of how this man in front of me made me feel loved, and special, and safe. Everything fell into place, and I knew Reece was the person I was to spend the rest of my life with.

When we got back to DC, we began looking for a home together. Whatever house we looked at, we'd imagine a child sharing it with us. *Is there a park nearby? Is there a Jack and Jill bathroom? Can we picture a child living here?*

Before children were part of our lives, the idea of them occupied this space in our hearts and our relationship. Before Reece had even walked across the stage for his diploma, we had already started to prepare. And we were ready.

I get choked up just thinking about him. He's my absolute rock, my center, my everything. I know for a fact that I would not be the person I am today without him. After all these years, I'm still madly in love with him. Catching sight of him across a room, having him look back at me, still makes my heart flutter. I grow strong from how much he loves me back.

Sometimes I just marvel at something simple, like how he interacts with our children. I'll see him at the kitchen table doing index cards with one of the kids for a spelling test or helping another one read, while also folding laundry and cooking. Thinking of others is just his natural state. I'm guilty of thinking of myself too much, I know, and I tell Reece he needs to think of himself more. But he just won't. If the family sits down and there are five pieces of chicken, he'll be the first to say he's not hungry, even if he is.

Reece is the liberal one in style and fashion, unafraid to be a little wild. I'm the conservative one, playing it down the middle, unsure of how to pull anything off with flair. I travel a lot for work, and he got tired of me calling him from hotels to ask what I should wear. Now before I head to the airport, he'll take pictures for me of which tie goes with which suit.

I'm grateful not just for what he does, but who he is: the most gentle, nurturing, and caring soul. The most positive influence on the children that I could imagine and the glue that holds us together. He's the organizing principle of all of it: the family simply doesn't make sense without him.

· 16 ·

BONDING STUDIES

November 2011

A year and a half after Amaya and Makai's adoption trial, we were back in court, trying to adopt Greyson and Tristan. That trial was not only more complicated than the previous one, but also more emotionally draining.

When the boys came to our home, Rose, their mother, was fifteen years old. She had given birth to Greyson when she was twelve and to Tristan when she was fourteen. At three months old, Tristan went into the system, and three months later, he came to us. That was Greyson's second time in the system, and since it was for a second abuse incident, the district was not recommending reunification; the goal for Greyson had been foster care/permanency from the beginning. Children who are in the system because of abuse, rather than neglect, get treated differently by the courts. At least, they're supposed to.

We approached their trial differently than Amaya and Makai's. For one, we were wiser about the legal ins and outs and felt more comfortable talking to judges and lawyers, like we had been broken in. Reece didn't testify in either trial, but I was more confident speaking my mind on the stand this time. The fact that we had won the last trial helped me stand solid in who I was and what I wanted for the children.

As Reece and I walked up the steps of that same courthouse, I experienced the worst kind of déjà vu. We entered the courtroom, which was much larger and brighter than the last one, with more light streaming through the big windows. Again, a retinue of lawyers sat at a long table in front of the bench.

Rose wanted custody of both Greyson and Tristan, each of their dads wanted custody of one boy, and Greyson's grandparents wanted custody of just Greyson. Various relatives also came out of the woodwork claiming to want the boys, but each was only offering to take Greyson alone or Tristan alone.

Again, Mr. Harris told us that we were not likely to win, but the one thing in our favor this time was that we didn't want to split the boys up. At the start of the trial, Greyson's father had just gotten out of prison for the statutory rape of Rose. On the first day of the trial, he signed over his rights to Greyson, but he wanted his parents to get custody.

During the trial, Reece and I had to listen to the horrific stories: how Greyson had shaken baby syndrome and bleeding in the brain as an infant, how Rose put him in the hospital with three broken ribs, how she tried to carve Tristan's father's initials into the baby's chest, how Tristan will have a scar for the rest of his life because of it.

Grandma Calfee had mentioned these incidents to us, but we didn't know the details of the stories until the trial. Plus, by this point, they were *our* children. The thought of them being hurt in any way, much less intentionally, made me sick, as though I could feel it myself. To know the suffering my boys once had to endure broke my heart into a million pieces.

One of the arguments that Greyson's grandparents made against Reece and me was that we were not properly bonded with the boys. We thought the charge was absurd so we paid for experts to do a series of bonding studies. The experts interviewed all three biological parents and the petitioning grandparents, as well as Reece and me, and watched us interact with the children in our home. The bonding study experts got on the stand and read their findings: no one had any bond with the children except us, and we had a very strong parental bond. They said neither boy had a bond with his father, nor did Greyson have a bond with his grandparents. With his mother, Greyson had more of a brother-sister bond, and Tristan had no bond with his mother at all.

The trial was long and drawn out. Rose fired two different attorneys, which added postponements that made it run longer than normal. During background checks on both of Greyson's grandparents, the courts discovered that they each had convictions of assault with a deadly weapon. After the findings, the government lawyer, the social worker, and the guardian ad litem went to the grandparents and said that even if Reece and I didn't get them, they would not get the boys because of their criminal backgrounds. So they withdrew their petitions. Soon after, Tristan's father signed his rights over to us as well.

Rose was the only holdout. She made it clear that she wanted the boys to stay in foster care, in a temporary situation. It was just like how she hadn't wanted us to take them to the beach (and later to Disney World). She was holding out hope that she could get them back. No matter how well-intentioned Rose's desire was, we thought it was selfish of her to withhold things from Greyson and Tristan. In the abstract, I had some sympathy for her desire to have a future with her children, but she never matched this desire with action. And I didn't think the children should have to wait because of that. None of this was their fault.

I was on the stand for two days of the trial. Rose's lawyer was just trying to grasp at straws to make us seem like unfit parents. She brought up my age (I was forty-five at the time) and tried to use it against me, as though I were too old to raise young children. Even our nickname for Greyson, A-Plus Boy, was used against us. Rose's lawyer claimed that it was setting too high a standard for him to reach, that it would ultimately cause damage and create self-esteem issues for him.

We had to hear her question our fitness as parents because of our sexuality, had to hear slurs and accusations from Rose that we were molesting the boys, had to hear that we had no right to raise African American children. The lawyer made accusations that because Tristan was light skinned, we favored him over Greyson—a baseless and insulting claim. After I talked about the bond between Makai and Greyson, how Greyson watched out for him, Rose's lawyer even turned that around on me. She claimed I wanted to adopt Greyson because I was just using him to take care of Makai. The most hurtful things came out of this woman's mouth.

There was no evidence of any of it, of course—it was all insinuations by the lawyers and hearsay passed along from Rose. The only provable fact was that we had done everything we could to take care of the kids.

The turning point of the trial arrived when Rose got on the stand. She had just turned sixteen, though she looked much older.

During her testimony, she said that she had a problem having two gay men raise her boys. The judge, who was allowed to ask his own questions, turned to her.

"When you first requested that the boys go to MS and RC," the judge said, "you knew they were gay, correct?"

"Yes," she said. "I did."

"So can I ask why you now have an issue with their sexuality?"

"Well, it's against my religion." This was the first time anyone had heard her mention religion, including us.

"You're saying now that you're religious, and homosexuality is against your religion?" the judge asked.

"Yes."

"What is the name of your church?"

"I don't know the name of it," she said.

"You don't know the name of your church?"

"I forget. I know where it is, though—on T and Eleventh Streets."

Later on, after the lawyers' questions, the judge again turned to Rose. "If I rule for you to have these boys back," he asked, "how are you going to support them?"

"I'm gonna be a singer," she said.

The judge looked at her, perplexed. "Wait—but do you have a contract?"

"No, no. But I'm good at karaoke."

It was astounding. Still a child herself, she was thinking like a child, like how kids talk about what they want to be when they grow up. Even after she had flown off the handle and said we were molesting her boys and the bailiff had to remove her from the courtroom, that moment just tore me up. I felt for her. I still feel for her.

●

The holidays were rough that year, as we sat around and waited for the judge's ruling. Reece had been maintaining the normalcy in all our lives, for Greyson and Tristan, for Amaya and Makai, and for me. I, on the other hand, was an emotional wreck. I kept saying to Reece, "They're going to take away our boys at Christmas." All I could think about was the worst-case scenario: a phone call, a ruling, the boys being taken from our home, never being able to see them again. The whole thing was like a nightmare unfurling before me.

About five weeks after the trial ended—in late December— after excuse after excuse, left turn after left turn, the decision came in. We again made our way to the courthouse to hear the judge's ruling. I gripped Reece's hand and breathed in as the judge spoke.

The boys were ours. We won.

The most overflowing emotions sprang forth from me, like a dam bursting. I sat on that wooden bench in the courtroom and just pressed Reece's hand so hard, squeezing the fear and anxiety and love and hope into that hand and never wanting to let go. The District of Columbia had finally decided to allow us all to become a family.

It's not that we needed the courts to tell us what we already knew. To make us what we already were. What we had already been for three years by that point. But we finally didn't have to fight anymore. Reece and I could finally exhale. I cried and cried and was not able to stop. We were saved: they were our kids now by law, and no one was ever going to take them away.

After the ruling, Greyson's father caused a scene in the hallway of the courthouse, screaming names at us when we passed. Other relatives, none of whom would step up to adopt the children when they were needed, were yelling in the hallway: "You stole our kids! You stole our kids!" There were veiled and unveiled threats, various slurs thrown our way. When it was over, the police had to circle us with marshals and sneak us out through a hidden entrance in the judge's chambers and out the back.

Greyson had come to us as a two-year-old, and by the time the adoption was finalized, he was a confident and opinionated first grader. When we met Tristan, he was a shy baby; by the time the adoption was approved, he was a joyful and boisterous toddler.

The day we signed the adoption papers, all four kids went up to the front and faced the judge. He asked each one to state their name, and they each responded, smiling and proud.

"Amaya Delisa Scheer."

"Makai Davis Scheer."

"Greyson Thomas Scheer."

"Tristan Rhys Scheer . . . but they call me Bubby."

I'll remember that for the rest of my life—how connected we were in that moment. But it also represented the final stage of what had been a choice on my part: I didn't let my childhood break me or let horrible parents determine the course of my life. I didn't let drugs chew me up or abusive relationships rip out my sense of who I was. I was choosing to break a cycle of abuse, for both my children and myself. I was forty-five years old. It had been a long time coming.

I had given myself over to love and was rewarded in the most incredible way possible with what I had always wanted: a forever family.

· 17 ·

THE POWER OF NAMES

Somehow, we weren't done yet.

The reality of the legal system is that it drags on long after the "end." After winning our court cases, we didn't realize how much further we had to go. Enter the appeals process—for both adoption cases. I chalk it up to the economics of the system; the appeals are a way for lawyers to ensure they get paid the extra hours. At least it seemed so in our case. None of the parents showed up to any of the hearings.

The appeal process for Greyson and Tristan took a year and a half to wind its way up through the court system, ultimately landing in the DC Superior Court, which was allowed to overturn the original decision. The three-judge panel had to hear our entire case again, but this time, Mr. Harris only had fifteen minutes to present it. Our case—our story and our kids' stories—had to be packed into those fifteen minutes. How could anyone communicate what those children meant to us, and what we were to them, in such a small window?

Even though we had been together for over four years, the appellate judges could've decided to send Greyson and Tristan back to their mother. Or they could have ruled that Rose deserved more time and sent the boys to a different foster home to wait her out. Because of the stakes, the tight time frame, the fact that it came at the end of an exhausting and tumultuous journey, facing that panel of judges was one of the scariest moments of my life. But they didn't overturn our adoption. Our family stayed intact. I could not—and cannot—conceive of the alternative. I thank God every day I don't have to.

But it happens. In the United States, it isn't even that rare. Courts regularly come in and remove children from their foster parents, or even their preadoptive parents, in a blink. In some cases, the children are being taken away from the only parents they've ever known, like property being seized. The courts then return them to their birth parents or drop them into yet another foster home until the parents are ready. No one can convince me that this is in the kids' best interests. It's unconscionable.

I recently got a message from a woman who had been fostering two little boys for over two years. The courts had ordered them back to their birth mother, a mother they neither knew nor remembered. This woman was just heartbroken; she was losing these children, and there was nothing she could do—foster parents don't have any parental rights. The biological parents can excise them from the kids' lives, which is often what happens. As a society, we don't fully understand the damage that does to a child.

I've met quite a few foster parents from all over the country and heard their stories, and I have yet to meet a single one (or even hear of a single one) who has remained connected with a child who was brought back to the birth parents. Not one. And not because the foster parents didn't want to be in their lives, but because the system is not set up to allow for that to happen.

I'm a believer in reunification; of course we should try to reunite families if it's possible, but I also believe the transition should be a healthy one. We can't just drop the kids back with their birth parents and expect blood to do the rest. Some of these children have no meaningful bond with their birth parents, having gotten maybe sixty supervised minutes a week with them. Meanwhile, the foster parents have been with them day and night.

The system labels them foster parents, but to the children, those are their *parents*. At least for that period. Our children came to us with trash bags and sad faces, and we did the best to give them a home, a place where they were welcomed, supported, and loved.

We need to be sensitive to the connection that develops, to the connection we should *hope* develops. There are questions to be answered: How can we partner foster parents with biological parents so children don't feel like they are being yanked from one to the other? Why can't we come together and make the transition a slow passage? How does it serve the children to tear them away like that? The system doesn't have to be this way.

Common sense says the exit should be a more gradual process. Going the other way—*into* foster care—we understand the need for incremental steps. Children are entering a new environment and obviously need the time and space to adjust—and the family needs to adjust to them.

When we took in Greyson and Tristan, we didn't just immediately move them in. We eased them into the fold of our family, from short visits to weekends to vacations to living with us. When children leave foster care, it only makes sense that we do the same thing, ensuring a smooth transition. We need to work collaboratively, as a community, to give kids a supportive environment. Let's show them that the situation is not their mother and father against their foster parents; it's everyone working together for their best interest.

Children are both very resilient and very smart. They will either build a different kind of bond with the foster family or eliminate it, but let's not make the decision for them. We have to let the children decide how to proceed—not the parents and not the courts. The entire system seems geared toward the best interest of the birth parents, which strikes me as misguided. If the birth parents had been looking out for the best interest of the child, the child wouldn't be in foster care in the first place. These children have opinions, feelings, and loyalties; they are not property to be shuffled around at will.

From my experience, the fostering period is drawn out for far too long, and the judge gives the birth parents far too much leeway. The reality is that about half of foster kids never reunite with their birth parents.[1] Reunification isn't even always the right word. A child like Tristan, who was taken away at three months, doesn't know his mother at all. We need hard cutoffs. We need judges who say, "If you can't get it together in twelve months, that's the end of it. Why should the children sit on the sidelines waiting for you? If you really want to raise your children, you'll get it together in this time frame."

All the waiting and dragging out just exacerbate the difficulty the child is going to have attaching. I'm all for being compassionate to these struggling parents, but with limits, and not at the expense of compassion for their children. The children are going through upheaval and uncertainty through no choice of their own. Letting the parents' bad decisions filter down to the children and then onward is only continuing the cycle.

•

I never had any connection or attachment to the name I was born with: Robert Chasteen. Chasteen, my biological father's name, holds nothing but painful associations, conjuring up loneliness, fear, neglect, and abuse. It makes me think of dirty houses, hiding in fields, cigarette burns, and the stale smell of alcohol.

When I was a kid, everyone called me Terry or Robert Terry. When I see my sister Beth or my foster brothers and sister, that's still what they call me. That's who I am to them. But it's not who I am to myself. When I entered the military at eighteen, one of the first things I did was take the name Rob. It was a small way of claiming something back for myself. But Chasteen still hung around me legally, heavy like a chain around my neck.

So when Mr. Harris called about the adoption paperwork, I was not about to burden my children with that history. "Can I put on there that their last name is going to be Chasteen?" he asked.

"No," I said, almost surprising myself. Reece and I hadn't really discussed it.

"Okay. You want them to be Scheers, then."

"Yes," I said, almost instinctively. "All the children should have Scheer as their last name."

When he came over for us to review the documents for the adoption petition, we sprung it on Reece, who was so touched to share a name with the kids. It meant a lot to him, though I have to admit, that's not really why I did it.

I didn't want to attach a name to our children that carried such ugliness. Once Reece realized how my name had been nothing but a burden to me, he understood. We were trying to revise the path of our children's lives, so the decision made sense. Names, whether we realize it or not, set us up for the future. They reflect a state of mind, of identity, of who we think we are and who we want to be in the world.

Two years after Reece and I got married, a few weeks before Christmas, I had been asking around for ideas of what everyone wanted as gifts. One morning over a waffle breakfast, Amaya turned to me.

"Daddy, I've been thinking about Christmas. And I know what I want," she said.

"What's that, honey?"

She caught me with those big eyes and smiled. "I want us all to have the same last name," she said.

I froze. *Of course.* The idea was so obvious—naturally my daughter would want that. I was the only family member who wasn't a Scheer. I was Rob Chasteen. My business cards were Chasteen. My driver's license was Chasteen. Chasteen was how I still marked my identity. And that fact kept my children at a distance—maybe not on a literal level, but on some psychological level.

Amaya's statement made me think about how my name had always been a barrier, a way to divide: My biological mother had a different last name from my sisters' and mine; my sister Fran had a different last name because we had different dads. When I went to live with Sue and Eddie, they, too, had a different last name from mine. My name was separate; I was never whole, never belonging.

So I decided to do something about it. I didn't want any part of that name any longer. I could excise it from my life. I had rewritten so much of my story, and now I could actually *be* someone else. Someone I chose to be.

For Christmas, as a surprise, I had my name changed to Rob Scheer. At the Social Security office, I walked in with my marriage license and asked for the paperwork to take the name Scheer. The older woman behind the counter was so genial about it. She was excited for me. "You know this is the first name change we've had for a same-sex marriage," she said, marveling at the way the tide had turned. "I actually need help. I'm going to call my supervisor over."

"Really? Is it a problem?" I asked.

"No, not at all, sweetheart. I just don't know how to do it." She laughed.

I presented my new driver's license and social security card to the family for Christmas. Reece was touched, and the kids were ecstatic: we were the Scheer Six. With that simple gesture, I was able to fill the gap I had carried since childhood. There has never been any talk in our house about biological this or half sister that or anything of that sort. None of that matters. What matters is our love.

Amaya didn't want a toy for Christmas. Or a doll. Nothing she could hold or play with or show to her friends. She wanted us to be one unit. The size of her heart and her compassion for others, which have only grown since then, just defy her age. In some sense, it's a validation as a parent. You wonder and worry about a million other little decisions. But when your child shows you how good of a person she has become, you can take a breath and be at peace with it. And at peace with yourself.

Not long after that Christmas, I passed by Amaya's room, and she was lying on the bed, chin on her pillows, sulking. When she heard me in the doorway, she looked up, and I could see tears filling her eyes. I sat down on the bed next to her.

"What's wrong, honey?" I asked.

"Daddy," she said, "I hate my mother."

It was the first time I'd heard Amaya mention her mother in a long time. And to hear her use the word *hate*, a word that we teach is as bad as cursing, was astonishing. Makai never brought up his mother; he doesn't even remember her. But Amaya has always had conflicted feelings. When she wants to talk about Nora, I listen. As Amaya got older, the conversations became more fraught, more painful, but ultimately, I think, more healing for her. Maybe for both of us.

"I know, sweetie," I told her, putting my arm around her and holding her tight. "Believe me, I hear you. I've hated my parents."

"I didn't know that. You hated your mother?"

"My mother, my father, my stepfather. So many people. I've had so much anger."

She made a face like I had said something strange. "But you never get angry, Daddy."

I smiled because she was right. When it was time to discipline the kids, I would try to get mad, but it just never took. And they knew.

I'd get revved up and say to Amaya, "No phone use for a month!" and she'd smile that smile at me.

"You mean a day, right?"

"Okay, a day!" I'd say.

And Reece would laugh at me because he knew that I would be lucky if I could make it even that long.

That day in her room I told her about all the anger I used to have, all the hate I used to carry in my heart. I'm very open with them about my childhood. At times Reece thinks I'm too open, but I want them to know. When I told Amaya that my biological father used to put cigarettes out on my legs for punishment, it upset her.

"It was a long time ago," I told her. "I'm okay now."

"I just never would want you to get hurt," she said.

"I know, sweetie. But once I forgave them, I was free from all of them."

She made a face like she didn't know what I was talking about.

"By forgiving them, they lose total control," I said. "It doesn't mean you have to like them or be with them or talk to them. It means you're free to live your life. You decide what your life is going to be. The whole time I was hating them and making bad choices, they were winning."

My biological parents had been dead for almost forty years, but hating them gave them this power—over what my life was and over what it was going to be. They had already made their mark on my childhood, my adolescence, my early adulthood, my relationships, my sense of self. I had to make a conscious decision not to let them matter anymore. My hate did nothing but keep them in control. I try to teach our children that there should never be room for hate in their hearts. Life is about moving on and not letting hate or anger eat at you and spread into the rest of your life. Forgiveness is about being free.

So I explained all this to my daughter the best I knew how. I told her that I had recently gone to my mother's grave. I wasn't planning on it; I just happened to be driving by the cemetery where she was buried. There was no headstone, so I went to the office to find her plot. Her grave has a thin strip of black metal with her name, and once I found it, I stood over it. "You know what? I forgive you," I said. "For everything. For allowing all that happened to me. And for knowing what my father was doing and doing nothing. I forgive you. It doesn't mean I have to like you, but you're my mother and I forgive you." The words made me breathe easier.

Forgiveness isn't really about the other person. It's about letting go and not letting the memories pollute you like poison. It's about moving on and not letting that toxicity spread and cause damage, not just to you but to those you come in contact with.

When Amaya and I got back to talking about Nora, the subject of choices came up, as it often does in our house. I think it's important for children to know that people do have choices, so I try to tie it into every serious conversation we have about mistakes, about our future, about how we should treat others and the responsibility we have for ourselves.

"But why did she have to make the wrong choices?" Amaya asked. "Why didn't she love us enough?"

"Oh, honey, it doesn't mean that," I said. "She does love you. She just has to worry about herself."

"I don't ever want to turn out like that."

"You won't," I said. "You won't. Just because we are related to somebody doesn't mean we're going to end up like that person."

"Yeah, but I don't know if I ever want children," she said.

"Why would you say something like that?" I was surprised— Amaya has so much love in her heart and is so nurturing to her brothers. Her warmth shines out of her like a light.

"I just don't want to ever make wrong choices," she said.

"Well, that's not possible. We all make bad choices sometimes. It's all about learning from things we've done wrong. Let's hope your mommy learned from the things she did wrong."

I refuse to ever lie to my children. I'm sure it's hurtful for them to hear how their parents didn't come through for them, but it would be more hurtful for them to think that Reece and I kept them from their biological family. They should hear the truth from us. I will never have them look at us and say, "Why didn't you tell us? Why did you keep us from them?"

So many times we shield our children from reality because we want to hide the pain, but the journey of our lives is coming out through that pain. We can't ignore it, and we shouldn't. It is part and parcel of who we are. We become stronger because of the pain, and if we can push ourselves through it, we'll find love on the other end. We need to have faith that our children can handle the tough stuff if we give them the tools and support to do so.

After I hugged and held Amaya, rocking her back and forth, she finally stopped crying.

It hurt me to hear her say she hated her mother, but probably what affected me more was the reason. I could see in my daughter's eyes and hear in her voice that her anger went deep. But that anger wasn't about how she had been treated.

"It just makes me so mad," she said to me, "what she did to my brother."

· 18 ·

HE'S MY SON

For years Reece and I both carried a copy of Makai's adoption decree in the diaper bag or our wallets. Before that, we had carried the letter from social services proving he was our ward. Sometimes we'd be at Target or somewhere else with bright lights, strangers, and long aisles, and he would get stressed and throw a tantrum—kicking, screaming, and banging his head on the floor. Everyone within earshot would stop what they were doing and stare, elbow, and whisper. The only thing we could do was pick him up, hold him tight, and get him to a safe place.

Strangers would try to approach us or stop me, thinking that I was trying to kidnap him. In the midst of it, I'd have to say, "It's okay; he's my son." That simple declaration: *This is for me to handle.* One time Makai was having a meltdown in the car, and people followed us to make sure we hadn't taken him. We went thro

lot of that. The world felt free to poke its head in.

During the entire foster and adoption process, no one—not the social workers, not the parents, not any of the family members— ever talked about Makai. He was the forgotten child.

"Are you sure you want this one?" the social worker had asked us. *This one*. Like we were choosing coats. "He's a biter. He'll probably never be able to talk. Or walk properly."

When Makai first came to our home, he couldn't speak, so he verbalized through acts of aggression. It's not like he was violent for no reason; he couldn't communicate his needs verbally, which is why he bit people. His aggravation looked to the outside world like he was just attacking people. He was locked in there and needed someone to *hear* him. Nobody wanted to get him help. There was talk of retardation, of autism, of a million other things, but the system wouldn't invest in figuring out the issue. They just wanted to label this boy.

DC Child and Family Services sent us to a doctor, who thought maybe Makai was autistic. Reece and I had done enough research by that point to know he didn't fit the mold of a kid who was autistic, but who were we to say? We weren't professionals. We weren't social workers. All we could do was seek answers and not let up.

When Makai was born, his mother brought him to a crack house, put him in a playpen with a piece of plywood on top, and basically left him there for eighteen months. When the police raided the house, that was how they found both him and Amaya.

Neglected newborns can suffer from a condition called failure to thrive, which comes from not being touched or picked up. Hormones and neurochemicals are released when a baby is held, and if this doesn't happen, the child doesn't grow properly. The baby is probably also not being fed right or exposed to sunshine, or so many other things that a baby needs.

Makai couldn't even stand, because he had no muscle mass. Babies strengthen their muscles by having someone help them practice standing. His tibia trauma, which caused his legs to buckle, stemmed from him not being able to stretch his legs inside his mother's womb, which had been damaged from her crack cocaine use and a lack of proper vitamins.

At the children's hospital, doctors thought Makai had fragile X syndrome, a form of mental retardation, because he had the large ears along with other signs of it, but again, no one wanted to dig into the issue. We fought to get him an MRI and genetically tested, which the district felt was not necessary. Even when we offered to pay for it out of pocket, we got pushback. When we finally won and the tests got done, Makai was diagnosed with fetal alcohol syndrome. FAS damages a child's growth, frontal lobe, and long-term memory, and causes impulsiveness and other maladaptive behavior.

It was like the key that opened this locked box. All of a sudden, the things we were experiencing with Makai began to make sense. It was a devastating diagnosis, but at least we were no longer searching in the dark: we had some answers. His issues had a source, and with this new knowledge, we could seek solutions.

We didn't know what Makai's future would look like, but there were few signs of encouragement or hope. For many conditions, there are medications, ways to facilitate the child's functioning. The stories we read about kids who suffer from FAS were just devastating and framed as though there is nothing anyone can do to help these children.

Reece and I refused to let our son's life become an inevitability, and we committed ourselves to working with him, even though we had no idea what the result would be. We just knew that if we didn't do it, no one else would. We wouldn't let the world give up on Makai. And if we didn't at least try to help him, we'd never be able to forgive ourselves.

To strengthen Makai's muscles, Reece would drive over to the day care every afternoon and move Makai's limbs around; at night I'd sit there in his bed and move his legs like oars in a rowboat. We would make him walk up and down the stairs even though he would have to lift his legs with his hands. "We're not going to carry you," we said. "You're going to have to walk, honey." At the beginning, our refusal to carry him was hard for him to understand. He would throw these unbelievable temper tantrums, but over time, he did eventually get stronger.

The doctors said Makai would never talk, so there was no reason to put him in speech therapy. We disagreed and fought the district until they finally gave in around the time he turned three. But he still wouldn't say a word. We tried to encourage speech by not speaking for him, by connecting his needs with language. If he pointed at something and wanted it, we would say to him what that was. If he wanted his sippy cup, we'd say, "Cup," and he would point to it and we'd say, "Cup," and he would point—over and over again.

One morning, when Makai was almost four, I was doing work at the dining room table when I heard Reece screaming. Fearing one of the kids was hurt, I went running up the stairs, and Makai was lying on the changing table clearly saying, "Dada, Dada, Dada." I looked over and Reece was crying.

Reece and I had prepared ourselves for the reality that Makai was never going to speak. To watch him say "Dada" was overwhelming, a bright spot in what had been a difficult year for him. A child's first word is a big deal no matter what the circumstances, but this one felt like a miracle.

All our children came running in when they heard the commotion, and we all started jumping up and down, going crazy like the Scheer Six sometimes do. *Dada, Dada, Dada.* We said it back to him in excitement, and he kept repeating it, this feedback loop that no one wanted to end. Makai's face, his crazy little smile, said that he knew he'd done something big. He could tell that he had broken through. "Dada, Dada, Dada," he said. And in our house, Reece is Dada.

No one is closer to Makai than Reece. Reece was the one who

was there for him each and every time: leaving work early or going in late to deal with the day care, never missing a therapy session, doctor's appointment, or meeting about his care or schools. Since I was the primary breadwinner and worked a traditional office job with regular hours and lots of travel, Reece was always answering these calls.

One day he came home and said, "I can't do this anymore. I just can't do it."

"Do what?" I asked, worried about what he was trying to say.

"Anytime I go to work, the only thing I think about is Makai."

"I know."

"And I don't think we're doing right by him," he said. "Or our family."

It was true. We were all barely getting by, including Makai.

"So what are you saying? What do you want to do?" I asked.

"I want to be a stay-at-home dad."

I knew how hard he had worked to get his master's, how being a designer was in his blood, how talented he was. "Are you sure that's what you want?"

"Absolutely," he said. "That's exactly what I want."

To this day, Reece tells me he hasn't had a single regret about it. I check in with him from time to time to make sure he's not feeling that desire to go back to work, and so far, he hasn't.

•

Once Makai spoke his first word, the words just started to rush out of him. He would call Amaya "Sissy," Tristan "Bubby," and after a few weeks of talking, he called me "Daddy" for the first time. Greyson took to it, realizing he was like Makai's teacher, and I'd hear Greyson try to teach him words. "Tra . . . Tra . . . Train," he would say, holding one in front of Makai. "Train." I'd eavesdrop on them and feel a swell of pride for both of my children. They had come so far.

As time went on, Reece and I started to learn what Makai's triggers were. We worked on directing him down another path so he didn't get to that place of anger and act out through biting, hitting, punching, or throwing things.

We had to remind ourselves—over and over again—that this wasn't his fault. None of it was his fault. Putting in the work and the time to help him was a way of saying we loved him and we believed in him. We refused to punish him for something that wasn't his choice.

When Makai was four, we realized the city couldn't provide what he needed; that's the main reason we moved out to Maryland, where the public schools were better, where there was more individualized attention and services.

So we moved to a suburban house with a yard at the end of a cul-de-sac, got another dog, and started anew. The kids enjoyed living outside of the city—playing in yards and going on long bike rides and exploring nature—but it was an adjustment for Reece and me. We had been city guys most of our adult lives. Some old friends thought we were crazy, but we just knew all the kids—especially Makai—would thrive out there.

Moving out of the city was the final step in a process that had been going on since the kids arrived: all of our straight friends and most of our gay friends—none of whom had kids—just dissolved from our lives. They knew us as the cocktail party couple, guys who went out late and were always up for a party or drinks. Our new lives just didn't appeal to them. I don't judge them at all, because I know it happens to many parents. You leave one world and enter another one. And you can never really go back. You never really want to.

•

Makai remained a biter at his new school, though, and now that he could walk, he was a runner, too. He had to be in lockdown care so he wouldn't take off out the front door. We didn't always know what would trigger him, and sometimes his meltdowns were so bad, his anger so out of control, that he would do things like break the television or rip cables out of the wall.

Reece and I learned how to restrain him properly, to do a "wrap," which is when we put our arms around him from behind and contain his hands, like a hug from behind. He would kick and claw and fight back. Once Makai reached a certain level, screaming and crying and thrashing about, we could not get through to him. We'd have to hold him like that so he wouldn't hurt himself or somebody else.

Over time, we learned to redirect him before it reached an irretrievable point. If I saw anger or aggressiveness coming on, I'd count down with him. "Count with me, Makai," I'd say. "Count with me. Ten—I know you can do this, buddy. Nine—breathe; you can do it. Eight . . ."

One of his triggers was not feeling safe, so it was hard for us to go out in public; we didn't want to set him off. Our lives revolved around what the family was able and not able to do with Makai. I literally had to pick him up and carry him out of stores or restaurants on a semiregular basis. We couldn't go out as a couple, because sitters were just not really an option. We tried it a handful of times, but the sitters always called us to come home early.

Distracting him was something we learned to do on instinct. Taking him for a short walk or holding and rocking him tended to work. After getting the school system to do an IEP (Individualized Education Program) for him, we found out he had a sensory processing disorder, which meant that he had a hard time interpreting sensory information from his environment. This caused him to react in extremes, both positively and negatively, which made it hard for him to function. Any kind of movement or pressure helps a sensory child like Makai. He loved lots of blankets, getting his arms rubbed, his feet tickled, and his back scratched.

Life with four children was already a challenge, but struggling with Makai was wearing us thin. There were times I'd tell Reece, "I don't know if I can do this," and I'd mean it. My heart was open to Makai, but I felt like we weren't getting anywhere. I wondered aloud if we were helping him at all: Were we failing Makai and also failing our other kids in the process?

If one of his siblings had a toy he wanted, for instance, Makai's anger would build as he'd struggle to communicate—he just couldn't get his words out fast enough. He had a tendency to blend his words together, so he wasn't that easy to understand. I could see his little mind going, but he was hard to decipher, which would just frustrate him even more, setting off another cycle.

Amaya or Greyson usually gave him the last piece of gum or slice of pizza, just to avoid an incident. As Tristan got older he did the same. But I worried about them, too. It's not that I wanted them to be selfish, but they were kids and it was okay for them to think about themselves from time to time.

Greyson took it the furthest. He wouldn't want to have play-dates, because Makai might get jealous. When other kids did come over, Greyson would go out of his way to include Makai, to make him captain or do something that he knew his brother could participate in. At one of Greyson's birthday parties, Makai was having an off day and Greyson let him blow out the candles. On his own cake! My son gave away the one thing all kids love to do—on his one day—because he was so concerned about the place his brother was in. There was something heartbreaking about that to me.

Makai had delay issues because of FAS, but he was also a devastated little kid. All this little boy needed to know was that people loved him, that we were there for him, that his family was going to make sure he was okay.

We began to feel like we had tried everything, and after a couple of years in Maryland, Makai was six and still not thriving.

March 2014

When Makai was almost seven, Reece had started reading articles and books about studies in which kids with FAS had shown significant improvement around water and animals. By this point we had researched and tried so many things: different schools, doctors, specialists, nutrition regimens, organic household products—there was nothing we hadn't explored. The studies seemed promising, so Reece and I had a talk. Then we sat all the kids down and told them the plan.

We were going to move to a farm.

•

We found a house on a suburban street that had a backyard with about two acres of fenced-in farmland, three barns, a garden, and a chicken coop. We knew nothing—less than nothing—about farm life. I knew that chickens laid eggs but couldn't for the life of me explain how those eggs came to be.

Just as we had with foster care, adoption, and Makai's special needs, Reece and I started educating ourselves. We didn't start slow; that's just not our way. We dove headfirst into the deep end. We read everything we could about how to begin, what made the best backyard farm animals, how to take care of them, the best way to use the land, whom to talk to in our county, how to turn a home into a homestead—a crash course in having a backyard farm.

The move to farm life was just as dramatic a shift for us as bringing four kids into our brownstone had been. We tried to make it an adventure, especially for the children, but I don't think it really sank in for them until the morning we brought home the goats.

I had only ever seen goats at a petting zoo. But the six of us got up one Saturday morning and drove to a huge goat farm about an hour north, in a more rural part of the state. There was an excitement and absurdity to the idea that we embraced.

When we arrived, a big woman in overalls and long gray hair emerged from the barn. I could tell by the way she came up short that we were not what she expected: two white guys getting out of a minivan with four black kids. She tilted her head in a way that said it all. But like with so many people in our lives, the initial surprise gave way to complete openness.

We briefly talked with her about what type of goats we were looking for, desperately trying to hide just how little we knew. She listened, then took us all through the field behind her house. When she opened up the gate to the pasture, the four kids ran in, with Reece and me close behind. There were droppings everywhere in the high grass, and there was a thick smell. About fifty goats of different sizes, ages, and shades—brown, black, white—surrounded us.

"These are dairy goats," she said. "And they've already been disbudded."

"What's that?" I said.

"Disbudded," she repeated.

I looked at Reece for help. "Their horns are removed," he half whispered to me.

"Why?" I asked.

"To protect them," he said.

The woman explained that the goats would have to be "redisbudded," a process that is like putting a cigarette lighter on the horn to solder it.

The four kids—all beaming and laughing—had huddled around one of the baby goats, kneeling down in the mud with it. "It's so cute!" Amaya said.

"Oh, I wouldn't take that one there," the woman said. It was a little goat, cross-eyed and walking funny, fragile-like, off to the side of the pack.

"No way, we want this one!" Greyson said.

"Yeah!" Makai added.

"What's her name?" Amaya asked.

"That's Lizzie," the woman said.

"Lizzie!" the kids yelled, treating her like a new baby.

"Lizzie, do you want to come home with us?" Amaya cooed.

Then the woman casually turned around to Reece and me. "I don't think you should take that goat," she said quietly, so the kids didn't hear. "She's a runt. Probably not going to make it."

We looked over at the kids and could see the love on their faces. They had all gravitated to this helpless little goat, and I could see we weren't going to win any argument.

"Looks like the kids want her," Reece said graciously. "I think we'll take her."

"Look," the woman said. "I can't tell you what to do, but that goat is not going to make it." Then she looked over at the kids. "Okay, how about this? I'll let you have her, but when she passes away, you bring the kids back and they can pick out another one. No charge."

She had given up on the goat, but my children would not. So we took her home, along with Callie, one of her sisters. The kids were ecstatic.

It turns out that goats are like dogs, loving and loyal pets. They'll get attached to people, come over to you, let you scratch behind their ears. When my kids brought Callie and Lizzie home, they smothered them with love, feeding them with bottles like they were babies. The children were elated, soaking it all up. Reece and I were mostly clueless, but we tried not to let it show—after all, it was an adventure. I mean, how many kids get to live on a farm?

Then we got some chickens—twenty-five hens and two roosters—and added some ducks. We read about heat lamps, how to change their bedding, and how to clean a chicken coop, which turned out to be one of my favorite things to do on the farm. I'd go out there in the morning and pen the coop, scrape it down, clear out every net, wipe down every surface, refill all the shavings and hay. I actually looked forward to the job; it was relaxing, a way to clear out my headspace.

We built fifteen raised garden boxes and began to grow strawberries and vegetables, so we could can our own corn, tomatoes, peppers, green beans. One of the benefits of having a big family is all the sets of hands, and everyone, including Makai, did their part. We got another dog; then we added a house cat, and some feral cats for the barn. We filled the pond in the backyard with koi fish and got two parakeets for Makai: Sunshine and Blue. Our home essentially had an open-door pet policy.

Makai responded immediately to the animals. He'd be in the backyard barefoot with a chicken under his arm, looking for the cats by the barn or running with the dogs, maybe swimming in the pond looking for frogs. He just ate it all up. I think he responded to the open space as well. At any given time he'd be running through the field, hanging in his hammock with his brothers, running over to the creek. After a few months on the farm, we saw a difference in him. He was able to start looking us in the eye and having conversations with us. He didn't mind being touched as much and was slower to react when something didn't go his way. It was a joy to behold.

After petitioning the county that the public schools simply could not provide for him, we went looking for a place that had experience with FAS, which had its own unique challenges. We found an amazing private school in the area that the state paid for. It was important that the school wasn't going to put our child in a box just because he had special needs. On our visit, they let us sit behind a glass window and watch a classroom. The small classroom had an area for the kids to swing from ropes, all this individualized attention, and three teachers for just six kids. Just by watching the teachers interact with the children, we knew it was the kind of place where Makai could excel, so we enrolled him.

That September, about six months after we moved to the farm, Makai started his new school. For the first time ever, he got on the school bus, turned around, and waved goodbye. I must have driven Reece insane, constantly calling and texting him. "Have you heard from the school?" I asked.

"Nope," he said.

"Are you going to go over there? Are you going to call?" I asked.

"No!"

At the end of the day, an excited Makai hopped down the steps of the bus, which had never happened before. He had ridden the bus both ways and made it the whole day without incident. And he did it the next day. Then the next. The transformation was magical.

Makai has grown so much. He doesn't bite anymore, and he'll let us hug him, which he never did before we moved to the farm. He takes medication and has the occasional meltdown, but he's able to get through his day.

Makai wakes up early Saturday mornings, plays with the animals, and then jumps on his bike and goes off for hours, and I don't worry. He hangs out at friends' houses down the street, or just alone or with his animals. Sometimes he just needs "me time," which I totally understand.

Not too long ago I was in the garden, and he was out with the chickens.

"Makai, I saved you some strawberries!" I said.

"What?" he said, walking closer.

"I saved you some strawberries because I love you."

He started running toward the garden. "Thanks! I love you!" That was the first time he had ever said that to me.

Life is very different now for the kids. They're allowed to want things for themselves. Any plans, like going out to dinner, once ran up against Makai's needs.

Now I'll say, "Who's picking dinner tonight? Tristan?"

"Buffalo Wild Wings!" Tristan will yell.

"All righty, let's go!"

"I don't really want to go there," Makai will say.

"Well, suck it up, buttercup," I'll say. "We're going." He's learned to go along with the flow. Simple things like that feel like a huge step forward for all of us.

•

Years ago, when Reece and I first moved in together, he joined an arboretum club. They sent him these two stick-looking things, which Reece planted in pots—a peach tree and a pear tree. For eight years Reece carried those around wherever we lived. Once we moved to the farm, we knew we were in a forever home, so Reece finally took them out of the pots and planted them in the ground to really grow roots. The symbolism writes itself.

There's so much to experience and to learn from on a farm. The kids help feed the goats in the morning and bring in fresh hay and change the water. My boys have started a business selling eggs to a regular client list of neighbors. The kids pay us for the chicken feed and then keep the profits. I like how it teaches them about business and self-sufficiency.

Right now, our children are forming their childhood memories. I think about that when I watch them chasing around the animals or riding their bikes to the creek. Our days are filled with love and adventure and silliness and work and joy.

I want so much more for my children than what I had. I hope that when they're older, our kids will look back and realize that their dads tried to give them everything. We want to give them a joyful childhood, an experience they can look back on fondly, something they can hold on to forever, and roots from which they will always be able to draw strength.

· 19 ·

JUST CHILDREN

December 2013

Now that life in our home had become steady, I started to look outward. It was like I was back on the couch all those years ago, drinking coffee with Reece, content in my life but disturbed by the news program about the foster children.

What seemed to linger this time were the mental images of those trash bags—the ones I carried my stuff around in as a child, the ones all four of my kids had been lugging from place to place, the ones they came to us with. Those bags were just baffling. In the twenty-first century, in one of the richest countries in the world, how could we still be letting children carry their belongings in garbage bags? The question haunted me.

•

At holiday time that year, I was trying to get into the Christmas spirit, but it just wasn't happening. Normally, I am all in on Christmas. We get two trees, and I always buy my children far too many toys. Admittedly, I'm overcompensating. I felt blessed that Reece and I have done well enough to provide everything possible for our children, but I didn't want to just feel blessed. I wanted to do something for those who didn't have enough for themselves. I wanted to do something for the kids that I couldn't bring into my home.

I was in my office making snarky comments to Reece on the phone about the toy drive we were doing at work, which felt very pompous to me. Even though the drive stemmed from good intentions, it felt like we were part of the problem: privileged parts of America buying some toys or a turkey once a year to feel good about ourselves. Giving is important, but this way felt so disingenuous because it was lacking thought as to who was on the other side of those gifts—what their lives were like, what they really needed. How could we actually help them? And not just check off our do-gooder box for the year and get on with our lives, but actually make a difference.

Later that day, I was leading a meeting with colleagues about the toy drive, and everybody could tell I was not into it. When I mentioned the facelessness of it, how impersonal it all was, and wondered what else we could do, one of my colleagues said, "You know what could help? You should tell some people your story."

It had never really occurred to me that my story could be helpful, that my past could be anything except a burden I carried. Or a nightmare I shut out. But that suggestion at work sparked some low-level fire within me.

That evening, I was talking to Reece about it and flashed back to the first night with Amaya, how the new nightgown made her smile. Then I started thinking about my first night at Sue's as a scared twelve-year-old and that unfamiliar bar of soap in the shower.

And a light bulb went off.

How scary it must be for kids in foster care to come into the system with virtually nothing. Nothing they encounter is their own, and—I know from experience—that starts to affect them, both practically and psychologically. So my idea was to put together some backpacks for these kids—filled with things they could use and love, things of their own. It seemed a simple enough idea.

Some work colleagues joined me, as did Reece, and we passed out flyers and put out messages on Facebook calling for donations. My company was a big help, and I had a friend with a radio station, who advertised on the air. We collected pajamas, blankets, soap, shampoo, books, and stuffed animals and put together five hundred backpacks, which we called *comfort cases*. The cases had a practical use, but they also sent a message: we were telling these kids what they need to hear the most—*as a community, we want you, and we love you.*

We delivered the cases to DC Child and Family Services and the National Center for Children and Families. I thought that maybe I'd do it again the next Christmas because it felt like a productive way to give, more than just a token thing to make us feel less guilty. A few local media stories appeared, and someone from DC Child and Family Services, the same organization that I had battled for so many years, asked me to give a speech—telling my story and how the comfort cases idea came about.

After the speech, a woman in the audience came up to me. She told me she loved the idea, had packed some cases with her daughter, and asked if I'd ever thought about becoming a 501(c)(3), a nonprofit.

"No," I said. "I really don't know what that is. Like a charity?"

"Yes," she said. "I'm telling you right now—you need to turn this into a charity."

"It's a good idea, but I can't imagine that. I have four kids and a farm and a full-time job."

"Please, think about it," she said. "Please."

So I went home, talked to Reece, and prayed about it. I could just feel that this was a threshold—one chapter of my life was ending and a new one was unfolding, one where I could make a bigger impact. The hard times I'd went through could actually mean something, could transform into something valuable. Adopting my children had been the greatest decision of my life, but I couldn't open my door to the nearly half a million American children in foster care. I had to do something bigger.

So I gave us a name, Comfort Cases, and turned it into a nonprofit organization. The next year, we did ten times as many cases—five thousand. The year after that was seven thousand. I set it up almost entirely as volunteer charity (there are one and a half employees), with 100 percent donations from the community and no corporate sponsors whatsoever. Volunteer groups began to come to the center to help out, and businesses, schools, churches, and scout groups started to do packing parties on their own—the community opened its arms so widely. I knew that people's hearts were big enough if only they found a way to show it.

As I write this, Comfort Cases has given thirty thousand cases all over the country, offering a connection to thirty thousand kids—getting the community to think about them, telling them that we love them and are here for them.

We've since standardized what goes into every case:

- A new pair of pajamas: because of Amaya, of course. I firmly believe that it wasn't the nightgown that made Amaya smile for the first time all those years ago. It was the fact that it was *new*, that she got to rip that tag off. She had that feeling that it was hers, bought for her.

- A toothbrush and toothpaste: because I have beautiful teeth, but I paid for every one of them as an adult because no one ever gave me a toothbrush.

- A bar of soap, shampoo, and conditioner: because the soap conveys a sense of personal space and dignity on those first scary days in foster care. Of course, foster parents' houses or group homes have soap, but it doesn't belong to the children. At hotels all the toiletries are wrapped because they want it to feel new, and just for you. We want to capture that same feeling.

- A book: because we want kids to develop a love of reading. A love of reading opens up a path to embracing education; it's a love that can change their lives, a love that can lead to so many other successes. Books, whether new or previously read, are the gateway to a different life.

- A new blanket wrapped in a ribbon: because Greyson said, "Daddy, we have to put in a blankie because they can wrap themselves in it and know we love them." He was six at the time. Like the pajamas, it's about having something that belongs to them. I want them to untie that ribbon, wrap themselves in that blanket, and know that as a community we care about them.

- A stuffed animal: because everyone loves stuffed animals, something soft and comforting to hug and hold. I have a stuffed bear on my dresser that my son gave me, and I'll keep it for the rest of my life. Like the books, these don't have to be brand-new. There's no such thing as a used one, only one that's been loved.

- A new journal and a pen/pencil set: we do this for children aged ten and older. An American Pediatric Association study recently found that foster children who journal achieve higher test scores than those who don't. Just writing at the end of the day, making sense of their experiences and world and having a creative or expressive outlet, makes a huge difference. I journaled when I was younger, and I hear from so many children in foster care who do it. For the younger kids, we give a coloring book and a set of crayons.

Recently we've started doing baby cases. When we began, we had cases for two- to nineteen-year-olds, assuming the babies were taken care of. But they're not, so now we pack baby cases that include a new bib, a board book, a onesie, wipes, and other items just for a baby.

One of my goals is to redefine what we mean by *community*. When people say *community*, they usually think of people they run into at the gym or store. Not about kids in foster care. The biggest misconception is that *community* means this zip code. But we're all part of the same community. All 438,000 kids in foster care are *our* children. One purpose behind Comfort Cases is to remind people that our children are living like this. The cases are for them, but they're also for us—as a reminder: *these are* our *children*.

If you don't know much about our foster care system, it's not your fault. In society, the reality is it's not something we ever talk about. That's why orphanages started getting called "group homes"—it's a way to distance ourselves from the harsh reality inside those places.

Until our community—all of us—knows exactly what the problems are in our system, we can't fix them. Our system is shattered and has to be rebuilt from the ground up. We've been making money on the backs of children for way too many years. We need accountability, we need standards, and we need to end labeling.

I met with a group of counselors recently and they asked me if they could start doing something today—*today*—to help foster children, what should it be?

"Stop calling them foster children," I said. "We can stop that now. They are children in care. They are just children."

•

I believe that the smallest thing, that tag on a nightgown, changed my daughter's life. Tearing that tag off on that first night gave her that aha moment. It let her know she was going to be okay because she was loved. Children in care are so used to being handed other people's things. They're given a trash bag with torn and tattered clothes and told to be grateful.

But it's not about the object—it's about the dignity and the connection. We're communicating to the children that there's a person behind the object—*someone cared enough to buy me this.* There's a person thinking of them, caring about them, worrying about them. When Sue first took me shopping when I was twelve years old, it meant the world to me. In group homes, no one is asking about these kids' days, no one is tucking them in at night.

Every person in this world has one thing in common: we all want to be wanted. The cases are a way to say that. I wish that we could say even more. Five percent of American children (10 percent of African American children and 15 percent of Native American children) will at some point be put in foster care. Those children are more likely to have anxiety, depression, attention deficit hyperactivity disorder (ADHD), academic difficulties, and behavioral problems. They are also more likely to grow up in poverty with drug and alcohol problems.[2]

Teenage girls in foster care are twice as likely as girls not in care to be pregnant before they are nineteen. Seven out of ten girls who age out of the foster care system will become pregnant before the age of twenty-one.[3]

According to the National Center for Health Research, "A close parent-adolescent bond is shown to delay sexual activity, increase use of contraceptives and birth control, and decrease the risk of teen pregnancy." Think of the love those girls in foster care are searching for, the way that desire can be used against them. The numbers back up how desperate these children are to feel that love.

Comfort Cases is based in Maryland near our home, but we are a national organization in thirty-six states, plus DC and Puerto Rico. At the center, where everything gets sorted and sent out, we have open hours for volunteers to come in. There are no age restrictions: two-year-old kids come in with their parents and help out alongside elderly retirees. Everyone not only learns what goes into a case and helps pack it, but they learn how the organization works.

When I meet with these groups, I don't want to scare the young children, so I talk a lot about our farm, how we have foster animals there and how they want a forever family. I talk about how it's our job to take care of them, feed them, make sure they have everything that any other animal has. One thing we do at the center with our volunteers is that we ask them to write letters for the kids or make bookmarks, to add that personal touch—to say that a person packed this who was thinking of you.

As Comfort Cases grew, I was glad we were bringing attention to foster care and cases to kids who needed them, but I couldn't ignore a basic fact: the cases weren't doing enough. They weren't a long-term solution, and they weren't eliminating trash bags at all. Kids were still using trash bags to carry their stuff because the backpack is only so big. We found out, too, that some foster parents had been taking the backpack, removing the items, and making the kids use it for school.

After an enormously generous gift from Ellen DeGeneres, we began adding a folded-up duffel bag, which we called a *comfort XL*, to each case. The comfort XLs—I believe—will truly eliminate trash bags in foster care. The emotional connection of the backpack is now supplemented with the practical step of the duffel bag.

So many of the children who enter our system do so in the back of a police cruiser. They are taken out of a dangerous and harmful situation and brought to a holding center at DC Child and Family Services or a crisis center. Sometimes kids sit for up to eight hours in those places. We want to make sure they get their cases when they first enter the system, to keep them occupied and to give them something to hold on to.

It's important to remember that no child has ever *wanted* to go into foster care. Even in the most toxic situations, they want to stay with their family—it's what they know. What's scarier than being a kid away from home and surrounded by strangers? Most people can't even imagine, but that's what these kids are going through, and we have to have the empathy if we're going to fix it. There's no other way.

We want these children to know the community that is looking out for them stretches far and wide.

Part of my work now with Comfort Cases is giving speeches to educate the public on foster care. Hopefully listening to one of my speeches will motivate someone to donate or have their own packing parties or spread the word. It doesn't matter how much money you make; it's about how you're impacting your community. *This is what you're supposed to do.*

•

My kids now live a pretty fortunate life, but I think it's important that they don't stay in a bubble. Giving back is a privilege and a lesson I try to impart as often as I can. They're all involved in Comfort Cases, and I'm proud of how generous they have been with their time and spirit.

If you're thinking you're too busy to help, remember: everybody can do something. You make time for what you want to make time for. It's as simple as that.

We're all meant to be leaders. No one has the right to stand on the sidelines and watch things happen and complain. You have to get into the game and change it. Stop complaining and start acting.

Action leads to impact. Whether you're five or ninety, you can be a leader. You can get in there and make a difference. Each and every one of us has that power.

· 20 ·

A THOUSAND WORDS

Because he was six months old when he arrived, Tristan doesn't remember what it was like before we lived together. He'll make comments about Grandma Calfee's house because Greyson and Amaya talk about it, but he doesn't really remember.

Of course, I love all four of my kids equally, but little Bubby is Daddy's boy. Once he got comfortable and knew he was safe in our home, he excelled. He was walking by the time he was ten months old and rode his first bike without training wheels when he was three.

Even as he grows up, there's nothing he loves more than to

curl up in bed and cuddle with me. We'll be watching videos together, and Greyson will pop his head in. "What're you all doing?" he'll say.

"Watching a video," Tristan will say.

"Nah, Tristan, you're cuddling with Daddy!"

"I'm not!"

But he is. It's his favorite thing to do. Mine, too.

Some nights he'll give Reece a kiss good night and then take my hand. "Come on, Daddy," he'll say. "I'm ready for bed." When we get upstairs, he'll say, "Three pieces of cheese in the orange bowl, please"—the night snack I've been giving him for years. He'll eat it, and we'll read or talk about his day until he drifts off to sleep. Those moments are worth more to me than just about anything in the world.

He's grown into an amazing and confident child. When he was six months old, we began cutting up and feeding him regular food because he wouldn't touch baby food. It happened by accident, but he's developed a really sophisticated palate. Now he eats things like sushi and raw oysters. He's an all-around adventurous boy, really big into skating, football, and basketball, and we have a trampoline in the backyard on which he does backflips, as do the other boys.

Even at three, Greyson was already a headstrong and opinionated little boy. He was demonstrative and expressive. When he was sad, he'd make dramatic faces; when he was angry, he'd make intense ones. He's matured quickly, maybe too quickly, but I'm impressed with how he's grown up. Sometimes we clash, but it's because out of all four kids, his temperament is the most like mine. He's very stubborn, in ways both good and bad, and he just commands a room when he walks into it.

Incredibly, he remembers life before coming to us, even though he was barely two. He can describe Grandma Calfee's house in detail: the smell of burnt pancakes, the blue daybeds on the floor, how she would gave them pink medicine to put them to sleep. He can detail the people who visited, what color shirt they were wearing at a particular moment, what the lights looked like in the convenience store on her corner. It's astounding. He talks about not being allowed to go down the street from Grandma Calfee's because "Mom's house" was over there. And that's how he says it: "Quote-unquote Mom's house." When he mentions his mother, he says, "Quote-unquote our mom." If that's how he needs to refer to her, that's his right.

He is a gentle and gracious soul, always playing nicely with other kids and treating adults with respect. He's always willing to help out, and if he sees that someone is sad, he'll go over and try to cheer them up. Teachers are always telling us he's concerned with everybody else's feelings. I think having such a young mother really affected him, and he's always been like the big brother in the family.

I love going to Greyson's basketball games, watching Tristan on the skateboard, or going to the park with them and Makai and throwing a baseball or football around. These are things I never once did with any of my fathers; I don't even remember sitting down and playing a board game with any of them. I do everything I can to rewrite that history, to be the father that I never had.

To have those opportunities with my children now is a gift. So, being a dad is one thing, but being a dad to a girl has been like winning the lottery. When I look at my daughter on the soccer field or in the backyard with the animals, she just blows my mind. She is wise beyond her years and understands that life is long. She teaches me so much and refuses to let the world get her down. I think back on that four-year-old girl with the sad face, who already had been taken from her mother and put in two different foster homes. We were the third, and she had no idea what to expect.

She has grown into a confident and outgoing girl, an honors student, soccer player, and horseback rider. And she's just a nice person, which is really what I care most about at the end of the day. I'm always saying to Reece that if we don't get it right with school or with screen time, all I hope is that we produce really nice kids who respect each other and respect other people. Amaya always makes me feel like we've gotten that part right.

May 2015

A few years ago, when Amaya was eleven, Comfort Cases got a boost in the most unexpected way. And it all began with a picture.

DC Child and Family Services and I had made amends, and they honored me—along with others—at a gala for my work in foster care awareness and advocacy. I have to give them credit because they have really changed the personnel and culture down there. They've been immensely supportive of Comfort Cases and have come a long way from the days when we first brought Amaya and Makai into our home.

In another full-circle moment, the person introducing me at the gala that night was Barbara Harrison, the very same journalist from *Wednesday's Child*, the foster care program that Reece and I saw on TV the morning we decided to begin this journey.

In the audience that night was a writer for *American Girl* magazine named Kitson, who approached me after my speech and introduced herself. "You know, the way you spoke about your daughter just represents what *American Girl* is all about," she said.

"Oh. Thanks," I said. I wasn't sure what she meant, but any parent wants their children to be complimented like that. "She's an amazing girl."

"I can tell," she said. "I would love to come and do an interview with her for our magazine."

The next day she called. Reece and I sat Amaya down and asked her if she wanted to do it. We told her it was entirely her decision. She said she wanted to, and what moved me the most was her reasoning: she thought that if more people read about Comfort Cases, then it would really help children in care.

Kitson came out to the farm to meet the family and all the animals. Lizzie, the goat that had been labeled a runt, had just had twins, which the kids named Oreo and Peanut Butter.

Kitson and Amaya sat on a blanket under the peach tree and talked for about two hours. She came back in and said, "Thank you. Your daughter is amazing. You've done an unbelievable job." She never told me what the article was going to be about or what Amaya had told her. On her way out the door, Kitson casually mentioned that there was no guarantee they'd run the story but that they'd be in touch.

Then Mattel, which owns American Girl, sent a young woman out to the farm that summer to do a photo shoot of Amaya and the family. Reece, ever the designer, laid clothes out for each of us, and he and Amaya chose a few outfit changes for her. The photographer took pictures of Amaya in her room, Amaya sitting with her brothers, and a picture of all of us: Reece, the four kids, and me sitting in the sunroom.

Unlike most little girls, Amaya never wanted an American Girl doll. When we went to New York City the year before, I so badly wanted to go to the store and buy her one. They're expensive, but I didn't care: if my girl wanted an American Girl doll, then she was getting one.

When we got there, the first doll she grabbed was a white doll. "Are you sure you want this one?" I asked.

She shrugged. Reece and I had been careful, trying to steer her away from white-skinned dolls because we wanted her to feel connected to her heritage.

"How about this one?" I asked, pulling an African American doll off the shelf. She didn't seem interested, so I took the white doll and said, "Okay, if you want it, I will buy it for you."

Then she looked at it again. "Daddy, I don't really want it."

"What do you mean? This doll?"

"Any doll," she said. "I don't really want a doll at all."

"You're kidding me."

"No," she said. "Can we go to Toys'R'Us instead?"

Her friends had the dolls and got the magazine, and we knew it was the "it" thing, but it was just not something Amaya cared about. When I spoke to Kitson on the phone, I was honest: I said Amaya wasn't a fan, and we understood if she wasn't chosen because of that.

Some time passed, and Kitson's editor called. "Congratulations!" she said. "We've chosen Amaya to be an American Girl."

"Really?" I said. "That's so great. But are you okay with her not having a doll?"

"Oh, we don't care about that at all," she said. "What we saw in Amaya is exactly what we think American Girls are. We were so impressed with her." Amaya was chosen as a feature story in the Christmas edition of the magazine, an issue seen by close to five hundred thousand people.

We kept it under wraps for months, didn't say a word to anyone.

A few months later, in October, a FedEx package came to the house while I was at work. Amaya called my office. "There's a box here from American Girl, Daddy," she said, "but I don't want to open it until you're here."

When I got home, we opened it up to see a small stack of issues inside. We turned to her feature story first.

"Do you want to read it?" I said.

"I don't think I can read it," she said. "Would you read it?"

I started reading the article, which I knew nothing about; I didn't even know what she and Kitson had talked about. The article was mostly about Amaya's volunteer work for Comfort Cases, which touched me so deeply. It took me forever to read; Reece and I just couldn't get through it without crying. Then we looked up, and Amaya had tears in her eyes, too.

"Why are you crying, sweetheart?" I asked.

"Because if we could help just one kid in foster care like me, then it's worth it, right?" she said. Amaya was only eleven years old at the time, but she had such a grasp of the big picture.

"That's right, sweetie," Reece said.

"That's what it's all about," I said, walking over and giving her a hug.

"Someone in foster care can read this and know that they can do it, too," she said.

I had never been so proud of anyone in my whole life. I was posting pictures, talking to anyone and everyone about my daughter. The magazines went on newsstands two days later, and I bought a bunch of them to hand out. My daughter was being recognized for something we already knew: she was a special, selfless girl.

●

Three days after the issue came out, a Friday, I was sitting in my office at work and the phone rang. When I picked it up, I heard a pause and then someone screaming, "You fucking faggot!" It was alarming, but I was more shocked than anything else.

Then I got a phone call from my friend. "Have you been online?" he asked.

"No."

"You need to look," he said. "Amaya is getting major national attention."

"For what?" I said, confused. "American Girl?"

"For the *picture*."

So I got online, and sure enough, it was everywhere.

A national organization called One Million Moms had objected to the photo in Amaya's article—the one of the whole family—because it was "pushing the homosexual agenda." They were calling for a boycott of American Girl and its parent company, Mattel. Their claims didn't make any sense. There was nothing about our sexuality in the article at all—the whole piece was all about Amaya's work with Comfort Cases—but that photo labeled Reece and me

"Dada" and "Daddy." That's what set them off. And they had mo-bilized people from across the country.

My phone at work started ringing nonstop, so much so that my assistant was coming in and taking my calls while I was scrolling online through these articles and comments that were saying the most hurtful, terrible things. As a gay, white dad who adopted four black kids, I had dealt with my share of comments, but this was far beyond anything I had experienced before.

Walking into my boss's office, I said, "I have to get home. My kids are getting off the bus, and I have to make sure I'm there. I don't want them to just stumble onto this."

"Of course," he said. "Take as much time as you need."

Before I left, I called the house and told Reece, "Don't turn the TV on or get on the computer with the kids around. I'm on my way."

I got home and just plunged myself into reading anything and everything about the supposed controversy.

It was unreal. Something that had begun so positively, that had made me so proud of my daughter, was turning into a slow-motion car wreck. Amaya's moment was being taken from her for the most hateful reasons. They were turning her story into fodder to hurt people, making it something divisive and ugly. On top of that, this was a group of *moms*, which didn't make any sense. Of all people, I'd assume that moms would be supportive of a couple who had brought children into their home and tried to raise them properly.

In the rush of the negativity that afternoon, all the old fears I had buried came back with a vengeance: *Everyone hates me. I'm a terrible person. Look what I've done to my children.* I felt like a bad parent for letting Amaya be in the magazine in the first place. I'd exposed her to this—it was all my fault.

The home phone started ringing, with strangers saying the most disgusting things to us and hanging up. Then reporters were calling to ask for a comment and bombarding us with questions: What did we have to say about the boycott? Was Mattel pushing the gay agenda? It was absurd. The article was about a girl who loved her family and spent free time helping out at her father's charity. How had this turned into such a bad thing?

I just wanted to hide. And I would have. But my kids were not going to let me.

The children came home, and immediately Amaya sensed something wasn't right. Reece and I sat the kids down and explained to them what was going on. "Mean people just don't understand that Daddy and Dada are two men who love each other," Reece began.

We reiterated that we love them and that it's our job to protect them and keep the hate as far away from them as possible. "We have a decision to make as a family," I said. "We can pull the shades, lock the door, take the phone off the hook, not turn on the computer, and this will pass. It always does. Something else will become news soon enough."

Greyson spoke up first. "But, Daddy, that's not what you taught us," he said. "You said if there's something wrong, we're supposed to fix it. We're supposed to fight it."

Reece and I met eyes. I looked over at Greyson and said, "You know what? You're right, Greyson. You're absolutely right."

So much of my fear and my desire to hide just washed away. My son was only eight years old, and he understood: Family means you don't have to carry it alone. You share the weight with others. Greyson knew that I was going to take it on, but he wasn't going to let me do it by myself.

Amaya agreed. At such a young age, my kids grasped a simple truth: we look out for each other. It's what you're supposed to do. As a family, we all decided we wouldn't hide: Why were we hiding? Why just sit back and let them do this to us?

No matter what successes my children achieve in their lives, this alone will always make me the proudest. When it came down to it, they understood what mattered.

"We're Scheers," Amaya said. "Let's fight."

So the next time the phone rang, we picked it up and it was NBC News. A producer told us that she'd heard about the controversy and would like to come and meet with us. That evening, the network sent a crew over to the house to do a story, and the next day it all snowballed: more journalists and news stations got in touch, talk show hosts across the country were speaking out in support, community members—people we knew and didn't know—were coming up to us on the street to express solidarity. The outpouring was more than I could've ever hoped for or expected.

On *The View*, Whoopi Goldberg showed the picture of our family and talked about how ridiculous it was that a girl loved by her parents was causing such controversy. The support was gratifying, but best of all, the attention publicized Comfort Cases in a way no planned campaign ever could have.

The experience happened in two waves. At first, we butted up against the hate and we had to face it. However, what we found in the wake of that was such love, enough to drown out all the vitriol. Friends and strangers reached out, telling us they supported us, that we were doing right by our children. Amaya became something of a hero at school, getting high fives in the halls, and random parents rang our doorbell, saying they were so lucky we lived in their town.

I'm a religious person, but I don't necessarily believe you should always turn the other cheek. Sometimes you have to speak out and right a wrong. It's easy for me to say that, though—I am an adult and that is my choice and, in a way, my responsibility. However, that's not a cross kids should have to bear. My children *chose* to make it their cross, too, because as a family we are a unit, and if one of us is under attack, we all band together and help out. We all must carry that weight.

My biological family was Southern Baptist, and then my foster family was Mormon. Reece's family is Pentecostal, and he had a few family members who were ministers. We both drifted away from our respective churches as we entered adulthood. With some time away from it, and after coming together, we discovered our faith again. We joined our local Methodist church, became regular attendees, and got involved as members on various committees.

The One Million Moms organization is ostensibly a religious group, made up of devoted Christians. Their boycott originated from their understanding of what God thinks and what sin is. As a religious person, I found their attacks especially painful.

Reece and I have a very deep faith, but that doesn't mean we're blind adherents to any of it. We remind our children that the Bible was written by people and that Jesus was an amazing person, just like Nelson Mandela, Gandhi, or Martin Luther King Jr. We don't spend time on the virgin birth or walking on water; to us, that's not the point. If anything, those stories can get in the way of the lessons sometimes.

The point is Jesus dedicated his life to bringing changes to the world that he wanted to see. He's an inspiration, having worked to bring people together, to show us how we must take care of each other. He left behind a legacy for us to do the same. As it says in Ephesians 5:21, "Be subject to one another."

To hear people who sat in congregations like ours—who read the same holy text and who prayed to the same God—say I was ruining my children's lives, that I was a pervert, that I didn't deserve to be a father, hurt me in ways I hadn't hurt in a long time.

That Sunday after the *American Girl* issue came out—and the ensuing response—Reece and I were on the fence about bringing the family to church. The previous few days had been an emotional roller coaster, but that morning when we got out of bed, we both agreed that church was for times exactly like these.

Our church is about 70 percent African American, mostly well-to-do people in their fifties and sixties, and other than us, there are no gay couples in the congregation. But they had always been so welcoming and open. When our family entered the chapel before the service, people were smiling and hugging us, but no one was really saying anything. I think they wanted us to be the first to speak about it.

Every Sunday, our reverend gets up and requests prayers from the congregation. It's an opportunity to raise a hand and ask for prayers or to share joys regarding something or someone. Our friend, a well-spoken man in his sixties with a white beard and glasses, raised his hand. Once I saw him get up, I knew he was going to be speaking about us. "There is so much hate in our country," he said. His voice had a slight shake, as though he had been personally hurt by the whole incident. "And we know that hate can fill people's hearts. But the Scheers—our church has opened its arms to the Scheers, because Rob and Reece, their whole family, are a testament to the power and strength of love." By the time he was finished, all of us were in tears.

Then our reverend, a tall woman with an impactful voice and a gray streak in her black hair, began her sermon. She has this power of speaking in a way that makes every person feel as though she's talking directly to them. I often leave church energized by her words. The sermon that day was about unconditional love, the path that people take to love each other, and how "Love thy neighbor" doesn't mean loving just the person who lives next to you. The true lesson is about loving everyone. She spoke about how we all should be driven by love, how we must accept others and love them unconditionally.

Then she turned the tables in a way that reminded me why we belong to our church in the first place. She said that love should extend not just to the hated, but to the haters themselves. When we hate reciprocally, we only perpetuate and multiply that hate. We do nothing but ensure that the negativity remains with us.

Then she asked the congregation to stand up and pray for those with hate in their heart, those who need to know that they are also loved. Hate is not natural—it is something we learn from other people, not something we're born with: it doesn't run in our veins.

Hate and ignorance are everywhere, in many forms, and Reece and I—and our children—have been subjected to our share. I've seen employees watch my kids walk around a toy store in a way that white kids are simply not watched. I've seen the kind of homophobia directed at me and my husband that would make you sick to your stomach.

A few years ago, Reece and I were out at the mall with Greyson and Makai, who were both seven at the time, and a stranger walked up to me and gestured at my sons. "Are they adopted?" she asked.

"No," Greyson said sarcastically.

When she walked away, I turned to Greyson. "Why'd you say that, honey?"

"C'mon. You're two white men," he said. "Don't they know where babies come from?"

We have heterosexual friends with children of a different race who tell us they simply don't get confronted in this way.

It had been getting better, though. In the years leading up to the 2016 election, I'd felt comfortable in my skin and with my family, even with holding hands with Reece in public. Both individual people and our country as a whole had come a long way in the Obama years. But since the election, the climate toward both African Americans and gay couples has changed. Bigotry and venom have been unleashed out in the open, in places that we normally didn't encounter it. Was that anger buried before? Was it triggered by our new president? Did the fact that someone so openly bigoted won the election make it more acceptable? I don't know the answer, but I do know I don't feel as safe anymore.

I always get more upset than Reece does about these confrontations and encounters. Reece is blessed with the ability to let it roll off him. "Just ignore it," he says. "Don't draw attention to it. What's the point?" He's right. I shouldn't spend energy on the minority of people who don't support us. But I have to admit they feel less like a minority these days.

•

The whole experience with American Girl, the fallout, and then the outpouring of love made it so plain: family has nothing to do with blood. Family is a feeling, a commitment to not let someone go through things alone. It's a choice to reach out your hand and to take someone else's. As an adult I've been creating the family I want, trying to rewrite the whole idea of what a family means.

On our first day at church years ago, Reece and I met this couple in their late sixties who lived down the street from us. They have children but no grandkids, and we just hit it off, eventually becoming so close that we all now call them Grammy and Pappy.

Grammy, who is retired from a medical career, is everything my children could want in a grandmother. If we need the kids to be picked up or Reece needs an extra hand, Grammy will drop everything and show up. Pappy, the one who stood and said a prayer for us in church that day, is a Nobel Prize winner in physics. He still works and teaches, but he makes sure he's there for our children, whether it's a school function or a big game. At birthday parties, Grammy and Pappy get there early, roll up their sleeves, and make party favors. They're at our door first thing Christmas morning, arms full of presents, ready to watch the kids unwrap them, to get on the floor and play with them, or to help put toys together.

What saddens me every single day is that my children never got to meet Rodger. Rodger, whom I loved like a father and who changed my life. I have pictures of him hung up at the house, and I tell the kids stories, but it's not the same. They would've loved him so much. Even though he's been gone such a long time, his ashes still remain in an urn on my shelf. I've never been able to scatter them on the beach like he asked. I just can't bring myself to do it yet. It would be like losing him again.

Rodger died with nothing, not even money for the funeral, but he did leave me Ricky. Ricky was Rodger's best friend from his old neighborhood, and when we lived with Mike, he was always over at our house. He's an animated and friendly guy who always lightens up the mood or any room he is in. Ricky has been one of my best friends since I was twenty-five years old; he's my kids' uncle, and they love him.

He's in his sixties now, fighting cancer and living with his bed-ridden mother. Truthfully, he'll probably end up moving in with us at some point in the future. Despite the illness, he's as sharp as ever, just as funny and street-smart as always.

Reece has his own story, and I can't tell it for him, but I know his parents have grown more comfortable with us as a couple and with me as a person. They're Midwestern conservatives, but they love me like a son, and more importantly, they love our children like their own. Reece's parents will drive ten hours to stay with us and spend the week with the grandkids—coming to all their activities and being part of the craziness of our home. For my children to feel the love—the power of this unconditional love—that was absent from my life for so long is all I ever wanted.

We have tried to keep a connection with members of our children's biological family who want to remain linked. Amaya has a great-aunt whose children—Amaya's cousins—have become part of our extended family. Grandma Toland is in her seventies now and still a part of our lives. We have become close with one of her daughters and Greyson has become friends with one of her grandsons, the two of them always texting each other.

After a few years of not wanting to come, my mother attended the Comfort Cases fund-raising gala for the first time last year. During my speech I wanted to thank her publicly and pointed her out to the audience. She stood up, and when I introduced her, I could see she was in tears.

"I'm so proud of you," she said to me afterward. "I always knew. I just knew it."

"Knew what?" I asked.

"That you were going to do something," she said.

When I couldn't see anything good in myself, when I was a shy and scared child just trying to make it, my mother had faith in me. She saw things in me that I couldn't see on my own. I know that she carries guilt because of the way Eddie treated me and because he threw me out, but I forgive her for that.

Our relationship is complicated, but our bond is solid because of what we've been through together. I will always remain grateful— not just because she took me in but because she turned me around when I was making poor choices and ruining myself. Without her, I would not be here. I know it. She saved my life.

As I got to know my children and embraced fatherhood, I thought about her all the time. Through the years, we had developed a good relationship, and she will always be my mom because she *chose* to be. As a twenty-five-year-old with a newborn, she took in a neighbor boy she barely knew. A boy with serious baggage. A boy who just showed up at her door one day. That is nothing short of remarkable. There's not a thing in this world that can undo that single act of grace.

When I asked her why and what it was about me that moved her to help, she said, "Because you needed me." That's it. The simplicity of that answer cuts through so much: I needed her. What more is there?

Her children, Nancy, Steven, and Blake, have all lived with me and worked for me at some point. They have their own families now, and we all try to get together so our kids can spend time together. They have their own lives, but we still think of each other as family. Just as Sue took me in, the three of them, as children, took a stranger into their hearts, and I will always carry a deep fondness and love for them.

My oldest sister, Fran, died years ago from breast cancer, and I miss her dearly. I have a relationship with her daughters, each of whom lived with me at one time. My other sister, Beth, lives up north, and she and I are still in touch; we try to talk on the phone when we can. The kind of bond we built during those years in those horrible houses is solid, like concrete, and because of that, my sisters will always be part of me.

•

Family is not something that you fall into or that is thrust upon you. It is something you choose. You choose to be in someone's life or you choose not to be. You make the effort or you don't. It's not about blood or proximity or race or anything like that. It's about what's in your heart.

THE FUTURE WE ALL HAVE

Where there is ruin there is hope for a treasure.

—Rumi

Since we packed that first backpack in my office conference room in 2013, I'm proud of how much Comfort Cases has accomplished and how far it has come. But there is so much more to do and so much further to go. The cases are just the *beginning*, not the end goal. The cases are a way in, to get the public to talk and think about foster care, to take action and alter the statistics. We need to change our minds and hearts before we can change our systems. *Inside before outside.* Change doesn't happen any other way.

One of the reasons I insist on putting a book in every backpack is my hope that it might spark a lifelong love of reading in a child. Maybe that child has never had a book of his or her own. Maybe that book opens a door for them into learning. I have heard education described as the silver bullet, the one thing that could change everything, and I agree. Education really is the difference maker, separating us more than color, religion, geography, or even economics. When I talk about education, I don't mean what we consider a white-collar education, either. College is a spectrum, anything from four-year liberal arts universities to trade schools. These all fall under the banner of education. We can't just continue to ship off a generation of kids to the military because they can't afford to go to college. It's cruel.

In recent years, I've been trying to expand our advocacy work to include children who are aging out of foster care. This touches most closely to my own experience as an eighteen-year-old, when I was kicked out of my home.

Shining a spotlight on kids in foster care is important, but when they turn eighteen, we can't just forget about them. The statistics for these young men and women are bleak:

- Only 54 percent of kids in foster care graduate from high school.

- Only 20 percent of foster kids who graduate high school go to college.[4]
- Only 3 percent graduate from college.[5]

And those 3 percent almost uniformly graduate with enormous debt under the guise of "assistance." On top of these challenges are the details we don't even think of: some college dormitories are open over the holidays and in the summertime, but most are not. Foster parents aren't required to take care of their children after they turn eighteen—mine didn't—so where do these kids sleep? Where are their meals coming from? These children are our responsibility as a society. We can't just send them out into the world. How can we hang on to them? How can we keep them in the community? I want to help develop a bridge for them into adulthood.

A few years ago, Reece and I began a yearly college scholarship for a child aging out of foster care. The first year we gave our own money, but now we are able to raise money through Comfort Cases toward the scholarship fund. The applicants are asked to write an essay explaining why they think they deserve the scholarship and what impact they think going to college will make on their lives. Reece and I, along with the scholarship committee, choose the winner. Then we present him or her with the award at our annual Comfort Cases gala.

In 2017, the winner was an impressive young man whose essay

was about coming over to America as an orphaned child from the Republic of the Congo, which has been entrenched in war for decades. The conflict has left five million dead, including his parents. He spent six years in foster care in Maryland, graduating from high school with an astounding 3.8 GPA, and plans to become a doctor.

Upon accepting the scholarship, he gave such a raw, truthful speech that the audience was hanging on his every word. He talked about how the system was meant to break people, but he refused to let it do that to him. He spoke of how he wanted to be something more in his life, and about how those people who have believed in him have given him the strength to pursue that path.

As I write this, he is now a freshman at the University of Rochester, in upstate New York. A few weeks ago, he called me to catch up. Then he started asking about how things were going with Comfort Cases. "You know, this year's gala is in May," I said, "after the end of the semester. It would be great if you came with us as our guest. You could meet the next recipient."

"That would be great, Mr. Rob," he said, "but I don't have anywhere to stay."

"What do you mean?"

"I don't have anywhere to live. I went back to visit my foster parents for Christmas, and my foster mother said, 'You're nineteen now, and you can't come back here for the summer.'"

I had no words.

The truth still has the power to shock me. This woman
been his mother for *four* years, wouldn't let him stay in
anymore. Not even for the summer. She was no longer getting the
check from the government, so she had no reason to. It happens all
the time.

So I invited him to stay with us at the farm for the summer.
How could we not?

This young man worked his tail off, overcame seemingly insur-
mountable odds, and got into a good school so he could become
a doctor. We owe it to him to help him graduate and move on to
better things. He deserves it, and my privilege is to be a small part
in helping him get there.

"You know, though," I told him, "just like the kids, you're going
to have chores on the farm."

He laughed. "Of course, Mr. Rob; I look forward to it," he said.
"Thanks so much."

"Listen. I just want you to know how much we love you and
support you. We are all so proud of you."

"I love you, too," he said, before hanging up.

The kids are excited to have another brother for the summer,
and like everything else, we'll make it work.

Ours is not the kind of house that is ever quiet. I know Reece
didn't think he'd be turning fifty living on a farm with four kids,
a ton of animals, and a fifth young person coming to stay for the
summer. And it's not like this will ever really change. We're never

going to be the couple that goes off to retire somewhere else when our kids grow up. This is always going to be our life.

If I had my way, we'd add on to the house and adopt tons more kids, but that's not going to happen. However, during Christmas and the summer holidays, we can at least open up our home, to next year's scholarship winner, to whoever needs it. I'm sure as they get older, my children will have friends who might need a place to stay, who might not have the best home situation. They might have to sleep on a couch or bunk with someone, but there'll always be a place here.

For those who are reading and wondering about shelters, I'd ask you to go visit one. Spend ten minutes there. They're terrifying places. They're overcrowded and understaffed, filled with addicts and sufferers of severe mental illness. As a scared teenager with nowhere to go, I chose to sleep in a public bathroom and my car rather than go to a shelter. It's no place for anyone, much less a child. Each year an estimated twenty thousand to twenty-five thousand kids age out of foster care, and many of them end up on the streets.

It's important to remember that living on the streets is not necessarily a literal thing. It doesn't always mean living in a cardboard box on the sidewalk. Sometimes it is, yes, but other times it just means having nowhere to go, nowhere you feel safe, nowhere you can sleep at night. If you're fortunate enough that you've never had to worry about where you were getting a meal or where you were laying your head, take a moment to think about how lucky that is. As a child, someone made the right choices for you. Now think about the children who are suffering because someone made the wrong decisions on their behalf. We cannot shut these young people out of our community.

•

Looking toward the future, I have three visions for Comfort Cases:

1. My original goal is still my primary one. We have to permanently eliminate trash bags in foster care. It's unconscionable that there are children who have to carry their things from place to place in garbage bags: the demeaning message it sends, the dignity it diminishes, the self-esteem it dampens, and the instability it conveys are simply not acceptable.

2. We have to educate the public about the foster care system and work to rebuild it. Until we accept these children and learn what their lives are like, we will never be able to help them.

3. We have to start making a serious dent in the awful statistics of children in care: the high school dropout rate, the college attendance and graduation rate, the prison rate, the homelessness rate, the mortality rate, the rate of suicides and self-

harm, prostitution, and runaways. Our college scholarship is a drop in the bucket; we need to mentor these children starting at a much earlier age. A mentor can have an enormous impact on a foster child, especially around the age of thirteen. Think about the benefits if these children had someone who could look out for them, help prepare them for college and the future, show them what life on the other side can be like.

I refuse to accept that it's someone else's responsibility. As a society this is *our* problem. These kids have no one else. If we turn them away, we carry the blame for what happens to them. Every single one of us needs to invest in their future.

Recently, I gave a speech at a middle school about giving back and leading by example. The students were preparing for a packing party for Comfort Cases, and the older kids were setting up a homeless tent area to spend the weekend in, to briefly get a sense of what that life would be like. Building empathy from a young age is so important for changing minds and hearts. Maybe they can inspire their parents, their relatives, their friends, and their teachers. When kids are giving back, learning about their communities, and figuring out how to improve them, then there is hope for the future.

That age group always has the best questions in the world. They ask things like, "Where did you get the resilience to keep moving forward?" and I tell them that I have a deep faith, and I knew that I deserved better.

Another will ask, "Do you feel a difference between raising children of color and what do you think it would have been like raising children of your same race?" and I tell them there is absolutely a difference. As a white, privileged male, I finally understand what that label means. Having three African American boys who are turning into African American men, I have felt a difference, especially in today's political climate.

The school talks also get my juices flowing because it expands the idea of learning. A school is not just for learning English, math, and science but for learning about your community and how you can make an impact. Foster care *is* your community. I tell these schoolkids that if they go on vacation this year, to bring their things in a trash bag, just to see how it feels. So they can no longer say they didn't know. So they can come back and lead by example.

When I speak to these young groups, I'm transparent about the bad choices I made in my life. I make sure they understand I didn't go from homeless to the navy to a comfortable life in the suburbs just like that. There were many years of poor decisions, dark times, and rock bottoms.

I speak about it just as frankly with my own children. They know what I went through—my drug issues, relationship issues, depression issues, money issues, home issues. But I worked to get myself a roof over my head and to get into a better situation. It took work, sacrifice, and deciding to do something with my life. I don't think I'm special—everybody can do it. Ultimately, I want to empower them to realize that they are in control of their lives.

I tell my children this often: Their mothers and fathers made choices, and that's how they ended up in the system. My parents made choices. Reece made choices. I made choices, and they make choices. It's a constant drum I'm beating—in both my personal and professional life—because I know it is a fact at the heart of everything else. Though I work as an activist and an advocate, I believe strongly in personal responsibility. I don't think it's a contradiction to have an open heart and also carry a belief that we all have choices. The system is shattered and we need to fix it, but it's up to each person to make the right choices.

As a society and as individuals, we can do something. Regardless of the problems we all face, they are nothing compared to some struggles these kids regularly go through: not knowing where their next meal is coming from, or where they're going to lay their head at night, or who loves them or if anyone does. Talented people, successful people, fortunate people do not have the right to sit on the sidelines and watch things go wrong and blame the system.

One thing I emphasize in speeches, whether it's to middle schoolers in an auditorium or to well-off donors at a silent auction, is that giving is not a responsibility but a privilege. It's a privilege to live in the era that we do, with the opportunity that we have in this great country to do what we love and ultimately choose the path of our lives. It's a privilege to be able to support the causes that we want and help those less fortunate.

Nelson Mandela said that everyone, regardless of age, race, or gender, has two things in common. Number one is they want to be happy, and number two is they want their children to do well. I think any parent would sacrifice their own happiness if it ensured a bright future for their children. Reece and I want Amaya, Greyson, Makai, and Tristan to flourish, to stand on lessons I learned the hard way, and to know the feeling of giving back more than they were given.

I hope my story and our work can empower those kids who are in the system and scared about what their future holds. Society may put them in a box, write them off, or assume they're a statistic, but I want them to know they have the power to change their futures.

Telling my story and helping others tell theirs is a way to let the light in to these dark places. I feel like we're making a difference—when we see a smile on a child's face as she rips the tag off those pajamas or when we get an email from a girl who has aged out of care and writes that my story helped her find the strength to keep going. That's really all we ever want to hear.

Our stories have enormous power. We each have a story that can impact someone else's life, whether we realize it or not. The other day Greyson was telling me about a boy who committed suicide at the local high school, which is just awful. The story broke my heart. I know that the right intervention could have saved that poor child and I used the opportunity to remind my son that *everyone has a story*. Always be kind to others and listen to them, because you can't imagine what they are carrying. Scientists have shown that holding secrets in is bad for your health—physically, psychologically, emotionally.[6] You never know how a supportive ear might help, the difference you can make just by listening.

•

Reece laughs at me because I'm always taking pictures. No matter what we're doing, I'm always snapping photos of our children. I have thousands of them, more pictures than we could ever look through, and I always order far more school pictures than we need. When they were our foster children, the district wouldn't let us take pictures of their faces. I understood the reasoning, but I hated the message it sent, that there should be no record of these children. In my eyes, a lack of pictures makes it easier for the public to ignore them.

The pictures are for me to treasure, but also for them, as a record of their lives. I don't have any pictures of my childhood. No one felt the need to take any, or if they did, no one felt the need to keep them. But children need that connection, and without it, they feel lost, untethered. The pictures are another sign that they are loved and wanted. As a society, we need to make sure that *all* our children feel loved and wanted. I can't imagine anything more important.

ACKNOWLEDGMENTS

I would like to thank Jon Sternfeld for helping me bring my story to the page. I'd also like to thank Chris Billig, my manager. Without him, this book would never have been written.

I want to thank my husband, Reece, without whom I would not be here today; my four amazing children, Amaya, Makai, Greyson, and Tristan; our friends and family who have supported us throughout; and my Comfort Cases community, the thousands of volunteers who have stepped up to ensure that on this journey I wasn't alone. For that I am grateful.

I would also like to thank Cait Hoyt and David Larabell and the team at CAA; Kate Dresser and everyone at Gallery and Simon & Schuster, along with Derek Jeter and everyone at Jeter Publishing.

APPENDIX

WAYS TO GET INVOLVED

Adopt a Child

Adoption changed my life and changed my husband's life, but let me start off by saying the obvious: adoption is not for everyone. If you are seriously considering it, talk it over with as many people as you trust and do an inner search. Figure out how you want to grow your family and be sure it's something you want to do before you take that first step. Do not go into this blindly. Build a team around you that can provide expertise, guidance, and experience.

If you decide that you're ready to adopt, educate yourself about the different avenues of adoption. Ask questions. Then ask more questions. Don't be afraid or shy or insecure: it's the only way to learn.

There are various avenues for adopting a child: international adoption, surrogacy, private agencies, Adoptions Together (which also finds adoptive homes for older children), and foster care.

Understand that these children never asked to be in the situation they're in. Do not make the baggage they come with—their special needs, their origins, the neighborhood they came from, their parents' education level or parents' alcohol or drug abuse—determine whether or not you adopt that child. Remember: there is no such thing as a bad child—just a child that needs a positive influence and some redirection.

Foster a Child

If you truly want to impact your community, consider becoming a foster parent. The word *foster* means to encourage or to develop someone's growth. It's not just about a house and food—it's about emotional connection.

Give a child the opportunity to know what structure feels like, what being provided for feels like, what feeling safe feels like. Whether a child is with you for a day, a week, a year, or more, you have the ability to impact that child's life. It is a privilege to have that chance and you don't know what that will lead to. You can make the difference between whether that child ends up becoming a statistic or a success. Every single child has the ability to achieve something. Your home, your family, the world you occupy can be a door opening for that child to a life he or she never even considered.

Imagine the feeling of seeing a child do something they never thought they could do simply because you believed in them. My son Makai was told he'd never be able to walk properly, and now he can do flips on the trampoline. It doesn't matter if you're single, married, straight, gay, black, white, or brown. What matters is that you have the ability to love a child.

For those who are worried, like I was, about the day that the foster child leaves, remember this: loving that child today doesn't mean you stop loving them when they leave. They remain in your heart, no matter how long they remain in your home. As a father of four kids whom society had completely given up on, there is not a day that goes by that I don't look at them and feel like the luckiest person on the planet.

Become a Mentor

Not everyone is built to have a child brought into their home. However, every single person can make an impact on their community. One way is by becoming a mentor. Go volunteer to help out or shoot basketball at a local group home, go take a child in care to the library and read with him or her, or offer homework help.

It will take time to develop a relationship. Don't be frustrated or feel like there's no chance you're making a difference. In the beginning they're going to tell you they don't need you. Why? Because they're used to being let down. That's what their life has been composed of: people letting them down. That means you need to work even harder; you will chip that wall away. Research ways to mentor in your community through private agencies or group homes. Find out where you're needed and how you can make an impact.

Volunteer

If you work part-time or even if you work full-time with the weekends off, volunteer in your community. If you have children, bring them along and make it a family venture. Teach your children to invest in their community, to learn about it and attempt to effect change. Whether it's reading to young children, helping kids at group homes with their homework, teaching older kids a skill, bringing over some homemade dinners, it all matters. It's not only the act but the intention behind it. You're making them feel like they're part of something larger—an interconnected network of people who care about them.

Donate

- I guarantee that you have bookshelves in your home filled with books you've already read, books that you never plan on reading, books that you will never read again. Who are you trying to impress? Clean out your bookshelves and donate those books. If you love that book enough to read it, then you should love it enough to pass it on to another person. If you have a child who has books he or she has outgrown, put them in a box and donate them to Comfort Cases. A kid without any books would love to get one.
- When you go to hotels, don't use their toiletries in the bathroom and ask for extras from the front desk. They'll give them to you. Take them home and donate them to Comfort Cases.

- Next time you're at a clothing or department store, grab a pair of kids' pajamas and mail them to Comfort Cases.
- Next time you're at the dentist and they give you a toothbrush, mail it to Comfort Cases.

Comfort Cases Center Rockville
15825 Shady Grove Road, Suite 60
Rockville, MD 20850

Have a Packing Party

At your school, community center, church, temple, mosque, or place of business, plan a packing party—see www.comfortcases.org for the list of what we collect. We will help you facilitate a packing party. Just fill out the contact form in the Get Involved section and someone will respond to help.

If you are in a school district or area that can't afford to do a Comfort Cases drive, you can still do a book or stuffed animal drive. We never call books or stuffed animals used. We call them already loved.

Be Imaginative

Everyone has something: money, time, a skill, a child who wants to give to the community, a love for other people, a knack for sewing or crafts, a love of baking. Think outside the box. We need awareness, funds, and committed people to rebuild our shattered foster care system. For too long we have turned a blind eye to this system. We must now face it and open our arms to these children.

ORGANIZATIONS

Comfort Cases

www.comfortcases.org

Child Welfare Information Gateway

www.childwelfare.gov

National CASA (court-appointed special advocates) Association

www.casaforchildren.org

National Organization on Fetal Alcohol Syndrome

www.nofas.org

Adoptions Together

www.adoptionstogether.org

National Foster Parent Association

www.nfpaonline.org

The nsoro Foundation
www.nsoro.foundation

The Annie E. Casey Foundation
www.aecf.org

About Comfort Cases

On any given day, nearly 438,000 youth are in the foster care system in the United States. Of the thousands of youth who enter the system each year, most arrive carrying little more than the clothes on their backs. If they are afforded the opportunity to collect any personal belongings, many are then given a trash bag in which to place and carry their personal items. It is a time of great upheaval and instability, and their first foster home placement is unlikely to be their last. Many youth in foster care will be moved from home to home multiple times, carrying their life's treasures in a trash bag.

At Comfort Cases, we envision a world in which youth in foster care are treated with dignity and compassion and where communities are committed to helping them thrive. Our charity's mission is to inspire communities to bring dignity and hope to youth in foster care. Our primary program provides overnight bags filled with comfort and essential items for youth entering foster care. Our cases are filled with pajamas, a blanket, a stuffed animal, a hygiene kit, a dental kit, a book, a fun activity, and a large duffel bag. Every item in the case is something that would have made a positive difference for either our founder, Rob Scheer, or his four children during their time in the foster care system.

Anecdotal evidence tells us of the impact our comfort cases have on the lives of youth in need. We have heard stories from many social workers and police officers about kids who arrive with nothing in the world but the clothes on their backs. Many who are taken from drug-addicted parents arrive in the middle of the night in soiled clothes. For some who have lost their parents and do not have a key to get into their house to collect any belongings, having a book and an activity to distract them while they wait for a placement is comforting. To have a clean pair of pajamas for these kids, a blanket and a stuffed animal to clutch until they are placed in a foster home has a tremendous impact. We want to convey to these youth that their community has not forgotten them and loves and cares about them during this chaotic and scary time they are experiencing.

We are committed to engaging our community to learn about the issues facing youth in foster care and to take action to alleviate their suffering. We also believe in the importance of engaging our youth to lead by example and encourage their peers to become involved with community support for kids in care. We provide volunteer opportunities for all ages so that the entire community can truly be involved together. To date we have been able to distribute thirty thousand cases through the kindness and generosity of our community. We have accomplished this goal without any corporate sponsorships and with a volunteer-driven force.

Knowing that only 3 percent of youth in foster care go on to graduate from a four-year college, we are committed to funding scholarship awards where we can to help provide better educational opportunities. In April 2017, we awarded $5,000 to a youth in foster care graduating at the top of his class in the STEM program at Cardozo Campus in Washington, DC. This young man began attending the University of Rochester in the fall of 2017 and is pursuing a premed degree. We also contributed $1,000 to the Montgomery County Child Welfare Services Scholarship Fund in June 2017, which was used to ensure that all youth in foster care in Montgomery County who are graduating from high school in a given year receive an award that they can put toward higher education.

NOTES

1   Child Welfare Information Gateway, *Foster Care Statistics 2015* (Washington, DC: US Department of Health and Human Services, Children's Bureau, 2017), https://www.childwelfare.gov/pubPDFS/foster.pdf.

2   Kristin Turney and Christopher Wildeman, "Mental and Physical Health of Children in Foster Care," *Pediatrics* 138, no. 5 (November 2016), http://pediatrics.aappublications.org/content/138/5/e20161118.

3   "51 Useful Aging Out of Foster Care Statistics," National Foster Youth Institute, May 26, 2017, https://www.nfyi.org/51-useful-aging-out-of-foster-care-statistics-social-race-media/.

4   Teresa Wiltz, "For Foster Care Kids, College Degrees Are Elusive," The PEW Charitable Trusts, December 7, 2017, http://www.pewtrusts.org/en/research-and-analysis/blogs/stateline/2017/12/07/for-foster-care-kids-college-degrees-are-elusive.

5   "Foster Care," Databank Indicator, Child Trends, last updated December 2015, https://www.childtrends.org/indicators/foster-care/.

6   "Keeping Secrets Is Harmful to Your Health, According to New Research from Columbia Business School," press release, Columbia Business School, May 8, 2017, https://www8.gsb.columbia.edu/newsroom/newsn/5187/keeping-secrets-is-harmful-to-your-health-according-to-new-research-from-columbia-business-school.

ABOUT THE AUTHORS

Rob Scheer is an advocate for children in foster care and the founder of Comfort Cases, an all-volunteer charitable organization that provides overnight bags, pajamas, hygiene items, activities, and comfort items to children and teens transitioning into foster care.

Rob started Comfort Cases and began a journey to improve the lives of foster children throughout the DC metropolitan region. After its first year, local companies began hosting donation drives with their employees, and Girl Scout troops, schools, and faith-based and community groups began reaching out to host packing parties. A 2015 *American Girl* feature article on Rob's daughter, Amaya, and her community involvement garnered extensive news coverage and national interest in Comfort Cases. The organization has since given out around thirty thousand cases and continues to expand nationally.

The Upworthy video about Rob's own story in foster care, the adoption of his children, and his community work has been shared and viewed over 100 million times. He has been featured in *People* magazine and the *Washington Post* and has appeared on the *Today* show with Hoda and Kathie Lee and on *The Ellen DeGeneres Show*, as well as many other local and national media outlets. Rob was recently chosen as one of CNN's heroes for 2018.

In addition to his work with Comfort Cases, Rob has over twenty-five years of leadership and operations management experience in the mortgage and financial industry. Rob is also a proud veteran of the United States Navy. He is currently the national spokesperson for KVC Health Systems, Riverbend campus, in which he advocates for children in foster care. He lives in Maryland with his husband, Reece, and their four children: Amaya, Makai, Greyson, and Tristan.

Jon Sternfeld is the coauthor of *A Stone of Hope: A Memoir* with Jim St. Germain, *Strong in the Broken Places: A Memoir of Addiction and Redemption through Wellness* with Quentin Vennie, and *Crisis Point: Why We Must—and How We Can—Overcome Our Broken Politics in Washington and across America* with Senators Trent Lott and Tom Daschle. He lives in New York.